Sweet Auburn Desserts

ATLANTA'S "LITTLE BAKERY THAT COULD"

Chef Sonya Jones

Sonya Jones

THE SWEET AUBURN BREAD COMPANY

PHOTOGRAPHY BY

Deborah Whitlaw Llewellyn

PELICAN PUBLISHING COMPANY
Gretna 2012

First printing, September 2011
Second printing, February 2012

Produced by Pinafore Press

Food stylist: Annette Joseph
Editor: Sarah Jones
Indexer: Sara LeVere
Historic photos, pages 11, 13, 1-17, and 19, courtesy Ann States Photograph Collection,
Archives Division, Auburn Avenue Research Library on
African American Culture and History, Atlanta-Fulton Public Library Stystem
Sue Ross, City of Atlanta Photographer, pages 20, 22

ISBN 978-1-45561-478-3

Printed in Singapore

Published by Pelican Publishing Company, Inc.
1000 Burmaster Street, Gretna, Louisiana 70053

Dedicated to the memory of my mother
Catherine Thomas Johnson

Thanks for sharing your cherished memories
And igniting my lifelong passion.

Table of Contents

Introduction

I was born and raised in Atlanta, Georgia, and I guess you could say that where I am today as a chef is a combination of my upbringing in this great city and the summers that my family spent on our 200-plus-acre family farm in Florida where my mother was raised. I grew up eating fresh food, meat, and vegetables, all grown on the farm—everything farm-fresh.

I remember watching my grandmother butchering chickens and slopping hogs. I watched her take the food to the kitchen and prepare it, and I tasted the wonderful recipes that came from her sure hands. Everything that she used in the kitchen came from the farmyard—eggs, pecans, milk, meat—all simple and fresh. We even had goat's milk.

Our best dessert recipes were saved for big family reunions in the summer when the whole family was at the farm. I was the second youngest of eleven kids so with all the other aunts, uncles, and cousins there in the summer, you can imagine the crowd we had around a table! It seemed like we baked from sunup to sundown, but us kids always had a good dessert with a meal and a batch of tasty cookies in the kitchen to snack on.

When my parents married and moved to Atlanta, my mother tried to hang onto her farm upbringing. She planted fig and peach trees, blackberries, and plums—all still there today—and this way she was able to duplicate the feel of that childhood farm right here in the city. Our house in southwest Atlanta had a little land attached, and we kept a large kitchen garden—and a mule to plow it! Mind you, this land is just ten minutes from my storefront in downtown Atlanta. We lived in the city, but it felt like a farm and we ate well because of it.

I have been blessed with having good things to eat all my life. As a child, I didn't think of the food we cooked as "soul food", it was just fresh food to us. There was no difference to us between Southern food and traditional African American dishes. The first I learned to cook was by

watching my mother and grandmother fix things. From the time I was about four—old enough to sit and hold a bowl in my lap—I was shelling peas by the bushel, and shucking corn. I loved doing these simple preparations, then watching the women prepare the dishes, and I emulated what I saw them doing in the kitchen.

When I was still little, about ten years old, my mother started a little cafe in our neighborhood called Cat's Corner. It was next door to our house, on the corner of Martin Luther King and Wilson Avenue. People could pick up a few grocery items, or get a hot dog or a hamburger to go. She also fixed fresh daily meals like oxtail stew, pig-ear sandwiches, or pig's feet, and always offered sweet potato pie and cornbread to go with it. I always wondered why people came to buy this simple food from us when surely they could make their own at home? It was an odd thing to me, but I think my mother's food was so good that her reputation as a cook became well known in our little circle of neighborhood folk.

Even at the age of ten, I assisted her in preparing the food we sold. She was my teacher, my inspiration, and my role model, and that's why I've dedicated this book to her memory. When she passed on earlier this year, people from our neighborhood reminded me of those days of her little cafe and told me they didn't know what they would have done without her food when they were growing up, it was so good.

———————————

Fast-forward to my education. I attended the University of Georgia to study fashion merchandising. I had worked in the kitchen for so long that I thought I might want to do something different, so I looked toward a retail career. I quickly realized that working nights and weekends didn't really sit well with me, and I didn't have the patience to spend decades working my way up to a management position. When I went home in my spare time, I always baked. Being from a large family had taught me that if I wanted to get my fair share of dessert, the surest way to do that was to make it myself. I had a keen interest in cooking that most of my siblings did not, so I was always assured of dessert!

My mind and heart kept coming back to the kitchen as I struggled with my career path, and I finally decided that I might use my knowledge of merchandising and my talent in the kitchen and become a caterer. I also realized that if I wanted to have a future in food I should get some formal training.

From my initial studies at the Culinary School in Atlanta, I was offered an academic scholarship to the Culinary Institute of America (CIA). I had to be real sure I wanted to do this because by then I had a four-year-old son at home. The CIA school is in Hyde Park, New York—a college town. I had never been to New York, or even north, but boy, was I excited! Somehow I made the move and managed it all. I studied for two years and received a degree of occupational studies in the culinary arts. By that time, my dream was to open an inn and serve great food and fabulous desserts to my guests.

But reality always manages to put some of our dreams way off in the future, and when I graduated and returned to Atlanta I had to get a job to make ends meet. I also baked and catered for friends and small clients, but I hadn't figured out how to get my business started.

Although I never thought to focus on desserts in culinary school, my first job in Atlanta was as a pastry assistant at Veni Vedi Vici Restaurant in midtown Atlanta. I created Italian desserts for that fine dining restaurant—tiramisu, and cannoli shells with marscapone, sherry, macerated cherries, and pistachio nuts. I liked working with new things because I looked at it as a challenge—after all, I was a black Southern woman hired to make Italian desserts! Since it was all made fresh from scratch, I was comfortable with the recipes, but I had to research a lot to learn the different ingredients. Oddly, when it came to procedure and concepts for the dishes, I began to see the similarity to my own roots. There are a lot of similarities between cultural sweet-tooth tastes, it seems.

In 1993, I was asked to teach culinary arts at Atlanta Technical College as a chef instructor. Most of the time, I ended up in the bakery. I had the freedom of creativity at the college and that became the spark that led me to understand that I wanted to specialize in desserts. The baking that we did at the college was the sort I loved to do. We cooked for the cafe at the school and I chose the menu—cheesecakes, cookies, and pies. Not fancy things, but from-scratch recipes that I so loved to make. I took things to the next level by baking the fresh bread that was used in school banquets, meetings, and at special events.

During the four years I taught at the school, people were beginning to talk about a "Southern food renaissance." I remember reading an article in the paper with a few chefs discussing a revival of Southern foods as an important regional food, and I thought to myself, "Thank you, Lord! Finally. Recognition well past due." At the same time, it was a bit of an ego boost to know that someone else was discovering what I had known all along: that Southern food was delicious and worthy of respect. I became more than ever determined to have my own business.

About this time, I met Edna Lewis who had moved to Atlanta from Virginia. I read in the paper that she would be at a reception, so I called the person I knew that was giving the event and asked if I could come and meet her. Apparently, my friend told Ms. Lewis about my interest, and she called me herself to invite me. I was very excited to meet her and

Founded in 1905 by Alonzo Herndon, a former slave, the Atlanta Life Insuance Company was one the largest African American companies in the country.

we talked and talked. Some time afterward she called me and asked, "Is this the teacher?"

She remembered that we had talked about my work at the Atlanta Technical College and wondered if I could assist her with some Southern cooking classes that she was holding at a culinary center in town. The classes would benefit the Revival and Preservation of Southern Foods, a group that Ms. Lewis spearheaded with others at the time; it was the forerunner to the Southern Foodways Alliance.

We taught Edna's classic Southern cooking once a month for a year and a half. I remember, I would pick her up and then we'd go shopping for food. She was very particular about the things she cooked. If the chicken wasn't fat enough, we'd have to go to a different store. In fact, we shopped at many different stores! We picked up lard from a store on Ponce, because it had to be refrigerated for her to buy it and some places didn't refrigerate it. She taught me why and how to be particular about my ingredients.

Our shared experience with these classes was a wonderful way to get to know Ms. Lewis, and our talks during that time were simple and wonderful. She wasn't afraid of butter, and she used it for the final touch to a lot of dishes, believing that it added much flavor to the food. She managed to put into words things that I had done automatically for years— things that had not been a part of the CIA curriculum, but were beginning to gain notice around the country.

The simplicity of Southern food reconfirmed the notion that there is a need to preserve the desserts and food I had grown up with. Food that tasted great and was good for you. It was a shock for me to realize in my years at the CIA that people outside the South didn't consider my food to even rise to the level of a regional cuisine. I knew what good Italian, Mexican and Southwestern food was because I had tasted and cooked it; but northerners didn't have the first idea what Southern food really was, outside of what they had seen in scenes from "Gone with the Wind."

For example, I didn't understand why Italians could take such great pride in a simple polenta, and yet our grits were looked down upon outside the South. They are similar dishes; and I had the notion—along

The market on Edgewood Avenue had been a farmers' market for decades during the Twentieth Century before it became The Auburn Avenue Curb Market.

Looking west along Auburn Avenue, with a view of downtown skyscrapers.

with others at this time—that it was high time our Southern food got some glory.

By the mid-1990s, the Southern food revival was full-blown, with Southern cuisine showing up on fine dining menus in many cities, and particularly in Atlanta. This, more than anything, motivated me to take the big step and open my own bakery in the Sweet Auburn Curb Market in downtown Atlanta in 1997.

The Sweet Auburn Curb Market was a fruit and vegetable market within a building on Edgewood Avenue in downtown Atlanta. The market had been held in that same building since the 1920s. I remember going there as a child to shop with my mother and seeing pigs and other meat parts hanging from the ceiling. It was a favorite place for local farmers to sell directly to the African American community and businesses near downtown.

During his administration, President Clinton designated this area an

Empowerment Zone to revitalize downtown Atlanta, trying to attract new businesses and customers to the downtown area. The Curb Market had benefited from this incentive, and the market now wanted to feature a wider range of businesses to attract more customers. In other words, it would be more than just a meat and vegetable market; it would be an upscale, updated food center for the nineties. A bakery was just the thing they needed.

I rented space in the Curb Market from 1997 to 2002, and named my bakery The Sweet Auburn Bread Company. I wanted to create equal parts bread and desserts. It was a chance to recreate my childhood tastes—sweet potato pie, egg custards, red velvet cake and cornbread—my Southern specialties.

My big break with the bakery came in May of 1999 when President Clinton visited the Sweet Auburn Curb Market on a trip to Atlanta. I guess I was considered a success story, having started my business as

part of the government revitalization process. Someone from the government called me and asked if I would mind participating in a round-table discussion with the President on the issues of small businesses. I was so busy with my bakery at the time, I didn't even get excited. I told him, "I'm real busy. I'll have to think about it." Well, it finally hit me that I had turned down an offer from the President when someone from the White House called me back and proceeded to give me all the reasons it would be beneficial to my business to talk to the President! I agreed to meet with him, and looked forward to actually talking with him about the problems of small businesses. I still hadn't realized that having a talk with the President might help my little fledgling business!

On the day they arrived, Clinton came to the market with a slew of dignitaries, Mayor Campbell, and Atlanta city officials. The newspaper that morning had run a front-page story about the visit, along with a picture of me holding two of my cheesecakes.

All I could think of that morning was "Oh, Lord, what am I going to serve him if he comes to my counter?" I wanted to give him a unique dessert that he would remember more than an apple or pecan pie. My cheesecake has a poundcake crust, uses fresh sweet potatoes, and has a unique cheesecake taste that I hoped he'd like. When he came to my counter on his rounds of the market, I had a slice ready for him and he loved it! Amidst reporters' flashbulbs popping, he tasted it and gave it a big "thumbs up."

When all of us vendors sat down at the table with the President to have our round-table discussion, the President sat next to me and introduced me as the "sweet potato cheesecake lady who was going to make him break his diet." That got a big laugh and made me happy, too.

Since that visit, the Sweet Potato Cheesecake has been my most popular dessert. People call me from all over the world to order it. Everyone lined up to eat what the President liked. The next year, Rachel Ray visited and chose to feature it in her $40 a Day show on the Food Network. That didn't hurt business, either. The Curb Market became a tourist destination and it seemed like there was a cheesecake media frenzy.

Recently a lady from Texas came into the bakery with an article from

The Sweet Auburn Curb Market as it appears today, busy and thriving.

The President tasting my cheesecake on his visit to the Curb Market in 1999.

Taste of the South in 2008. She had saved it so she would remember to visit the bakery when she came to town. Those kind of customers really make a small business owner proud! I never dreamed that my desserts would draw fans from all over the country.

Of course, I soon realized that the Curb Market was not a big enough space for the kind of baking that I wanted to do. In 2002 I had an opportunity to move back to my old neighborhood where I grew up to run a little restaurant. I was only there a couple of years before the owner of the building decided he wanted to tear it down and build something else. I felt it was time to move downtown again.

I had always wanted to be a part of the Sweet Auburn District along Auburn Avenue. I wanted to be part of the community of African American businesses on the street that had such an important and vibrant history in the South. Luckily, I found a spot at 234 Auburn Avenue, just one street over from the Curb Market.

The name "Sweet Auburn" is magic to African Americans who know its

Politics and churches have co-existed along Auburn Avenue for a century.

history. The street was originally named Wheat Street and the location was used by the Union army to quarter troops during the Civil War. After the war, the area developed quickly because of the proximity to the railroad and the black communities that grew up around there, and in 1893 the name of the street was changed to Auburn Avenue.

The mile-and-a-half-long street has seen more financial institutions, professionals, educators, entertainers, and politicians than any other African American street in the South. The name "Sweet Auburn" was coined by John Wesley Dobbs, who referred to Auburn Avenue as "the richest Negro street in the world." (Dobbs' grandson, Maynard Jackson, became the first African American mayor of Atlanta.) Because of Jim Crow laws, many African Americans established businesses, congregations and social organizations here, close to residential black communities of the time.

From the 1920s to the 1940s, Sweet Auburn was at the height of its social and financial vigor. The Citizens Trust Bank, Mutual Federal Sav-

Along with the tourists, the Sweet Auburn Curb Market remains the go-to place for locals to shop for fresh produce.

ings & Loan, and the Atlanta Life Insurance Company—the latter, founded by a former slave from Walton County, Georgia, was the second largest black insurance company in the United States—were all located on Auburn Avenue. Top Hat, the famous ragtime club that opened in 1938 and hosted entertainers such as B.B. King, the Four Tops, the Tams, and Gladys Knight; the Rucker Building, Atlanta's first black-owned office building, constructed in 1904; and the Martin Luther King Center are all part of Sweet Auburn's history, success, and charm. Several churches are also located along the avenue and maintain the feeling of community. Big Bethel African Methodist Episcopal Church, and First Congregational are part of the history of the area.

The Martin Luther King Center has brought visitors from all the world to Auburn Avenue to visit his burial site and learn about the work he did during his lifetime.

Although the area suffered from crime and abandonment in the latter part of the 20th century, Auburn Avenue was designated a national historic landmark in 1976 and has since begun to thrive, as commerce and culture are once again at the epicenter of Auburn Avenue. Today, the street is alive with tourists and commerce has picked up, due to revitalization efforts and the popularity of the Sweet Auburn Spring Fest, The Martin Luther King, Jr. March and Rally, the Black History Month Parade, the Sweet Auburn Curb Market, and the Martin Luther King Center.

Locating the Sweet Auburn Bread Company on Auburn Avenue was a dream come true for this native Atlantan, and I quickly went to work on the menu of desserts and breads I wanted to offer at the new storefront.

I knew I wanted to create heritage desserts and I thought back to my days with Edna Lewis. She and I had long conversations about food, and she gave me a book that has influenced me greatly. The book was *What Mrs. Fisher Knows about Old Southern Cooking,* which was written in 1881 by a former slave who had gained fame as a cook when she moved to San Francisco where she created a business selling pickles, sauces, jellies and preserves.

Ms. Lewis and I talked about Mrs. Fisher's book at length, and what came out of our discussions was a decision to feature a blackberry roly poly, a very old-fashioned dessert, that we put on the class menu to teach. It was such a success that we chose to teach more of the heritage desserts in our classes.

Mrs. Fisher's little book really charmed and inspired me. She couldn't even write—her friends wrote the recipes down as she dictated them—but her skill and talent validates African American cooks to this day. Their knowledge used to be passed down by word of mouth, but she was the first and one true voice for African American cooks. Interestingly, the book was a success with both a white and black audience, such was Mrs. Fisher's fame. I often wonder what motivated her to write down these recipes, but I'm glad that her knowledge has been preserved, and I'm sure she felt that it was important to pass this knowledge on to others who had her needs and limitations. It helps me to realize that there is a very real need for what I do and what I say, which is to preserve and update some of the heritage desserts I know. Sharing these recipes is a gift back for all that has been done for me over the years, and I'm happy to know that others might enjoy the poundcakes, roly polys, tassies, and stack cakes that are part of our childhood experience.

I really love to get feedback from my customers. One customer recently told me they haven't had an egg custard since a great aunt made it for them twenty years ago and it was exciting to find the taste again. Young people don't seem to have a clue about what heritage recipes are, but they recognize the taste or look of something their grandmother might have made for them. I think the sense of taste is tied directly to our memory, don't you? What I do with heritage recipes is the same thing

my mother did when she cooked cornbread and sold it at her little store. The neighbors came and bought her cornbread not because it was so special and different, but because it was fresh and cooked in a way that reminded them of what cornbread should be! I like to think that my desserts offer that same "taste memory" for customers and for those of you who try some of these recipes.

I describe heritage desserts as ones that are passed down and embraced by the cultures that claim the origins of the recipes. Each culture has a special history of food that is a part of a larger regional cuisine—just as African American food is a part of the larger Southern food experience.

We open the doors to the bakery at 7 a.m. for the business people on the street who want to get muffins and coffee, buttermilk biscuits with smoked sausage, a pie to take to the office, or a platter of biscuits for a big meeting they might have—whatever. In the mornings, a lot of people we know stop by as part of their routine. We also get tourists who come through on their way to the King Center. For these people, it might be their first introduction to Southern cuisine. They taste their first sweet potato muffin and they find it an intriguing taste—and good, too! It's interesting to see international visitors discover our desserts for the first time.

Like the customers who come through my doors, you may taste something that you find familiar in the recipes on these pages, or you may be experiencing some of these tastes for the first time. Whatever your history is with these desserts, I hope that you enjoy them as much as I enjoy sharing them with you. And I also hope you see a little of the love and history that is stirred into all these recipes. They come from my heart. Pass them on, share them… that way we can be sure that we will always have them.

That is my hope and my joy.

—*Chef Sonya Jones*

Coconut cream pie

Serves 8

1 pie shell, prebaked (see recipe, p.36)

Filling
1 cup white sugar
1/4 cup cornstarch
1/4 teaspoon salt
3 cups milk
4 egg yolks
1 1/2 teaspoons vanilla extract

2 tablespoons (1/4 stick) butter
1 cup coconut flakes, plus 1/4 cup
  for garnish

Whipped Cream Topping
1 cup whipping cream
1/2 cup powdered sugar

In a medium saucepan over medium heat, combine the sugar, cornstarch, and salt and gradually add in the milk. Mix until the cornstarch dissolves completely and cook until the mixture comes to a boil, stirring continuously.

In a separate bowl, beat the egg yolks slightly, and gradually stir 1 cup of the hot milk into the yolks. Return the egg mixture to the saucepan and bring to a gentle boil. Reduce the heat to low and cook 2 minutes more. Remove the pan from the heat and stir in the vanilla and butter, then add the coconut.

Pour the hot filling mixture into the baked, cooled pie crust and allow the filling to cool. Cover the pie and chill until the filling has set.

To make the whipped cream, beat the whipping cream until it becomes foamy. Gradually add the powdered sugar, beating until soft peaks form. Spread the whipped cream over the chilled pie.

To toast the cococnut, preheat the oven to 350 degrees F. Spread 1/4 cup coconut flakes on a rimmed baking sheet and bake 5 to 10 minutes, stirring occasionally, or until the coconut turns golden.

Garnish the top with toasted coconut before serving.

Buttermilk lemon chess pie

Serves 8

1 pie shell (see recipe, p.36)

Filling
2 cups white sugar
1 tablespoon flour
1 tablespoon cornmeal
1/4 teaspoon salt
1 tablespoon lemon zest

1/4 cup fresh squeezed lemon juice
1/4 cup buttermilk
4 eggs, beaten
4 tablespoons (1/2 stick) butter,
   melted

Garnish
Fresh blackberries

Preheat the oven to 350 degrees F.

In a large mixing bowl combine the sugar, flour, cornmeal, and salt. Add the lemon zest, lemon juice, and buttermilk and mix thoroughly. Add the eggs and butter and mix until smooth.

Pour the filling into an unbaked pie shell. Bake for 45 minutes, or until set in the center. Allow the pie to cool completely and garnish with fresh blackberries or seasonal fruit before serving.

Old-fashioned egg custard pie

Serves 8

1 pie shell (see recipe, p.36)

Filling
4 eggs, beaten
3/4 cup white sugar
1/4 teaspoon salt

1/4 teaspoon fresh ground nutmeg,
    plus more for garnish
2 cups milk
1/2 cup half and half
1 teaspoon vanilla extract

Preheat the oven to 400 degrees F.

In a medium mixing bowl stir together the eggs, sugar, salt, and nutmeg until well blended. Gradually stir in the milk, half and half, and vanilla and mix well.

Pour the custard into the unbaked pie shell. Sprinkle the custard with the additional nutmeg. Bake at 400 degrees F for 15 minutes, then reduce the temperature to 350 degrees F and bake for 35 minutes more, or until a knife inserted in the center comes out clean.

Allow the pie to cool completely, then refrigerate until ready to serve.

Southern pecan pie

Serves 8

1 pie shell (see recipe, p.36)

Filling
1 cup sugar
Pinch salt

1 cup corn syrup
4 eggs
8 tablespoons (1 stick) butter,
  melted
1 teaspoon vanilla extract
1 1/2 cups pecans, chopped

Preheat the oven to 350 degrees F.

In a large bowl combine the sugar, salt, and corn syrup. Add the eggs one at a time. Stir in the melted butter and vanilla. Spread the pecans in the bottom of an unbaked pie shell and pour the filling over the pecans.

Bake for 45 to 55 minutes, or until the filling has set and a toothpick inserted in the middle comes out clean.

Pie pastry dough

Yields 1 (9-inch) pie shell

1 1/2 cups flour
1/2 teaspoon salt
2 tablespoons shortening
4 tablespoonss (1/2 stick) butter
1/2 cup cold water

To make the pastry dough, mix the flour and salt together in a mixing bowl. Cut in the shortening and butter with a pastry blender or fork until the mixture has the texture of coarse cornmeal. Add the cold water and mix until the dough is consistently moistened. Shape the dough into a ball and press flat. Wrap the dough in plastic and refrigerate for at least 30 minutes. Once the dough has chilled, roll it out on a lightly floured surface to a 1/2-inch thickness. Transfer the dough to a 9-inch pie pan and trim the edges. Use a pastry crimper to make decorative edges, if desired.

To prebake a pie shell, preheat the oven to 425 degrees F. Using a fork, prick holes in the bottom and sides of the pie shell. Bake for 10 to 12 minutes, or until the crust is golden brown.

NOTE: To make a chocolate pastry dough, add 1 tablespoon of cocoa powder and 1 tablespoon of water to the above recipe.

Double crust pie pastry dough

Yields 2 (9-inch) pie shells

3 cups all-purpose flour
2 1/2 teaspoons sugar
3/4 teaspoon salt
2/3 cup vegetable shortening,
    chilled and cut into pieces

10 tablespoons (1 1/4 sticks)
    unsalted butter, chilled and cut
    into pieces
10 tablespoons ice water, or as
    needed to form dough

To make the pastry dough, combine the flour, sugar, and salt in a large mixing bowl. Using a pastry blender or fork, cut in the shortening and butter until a course meal forms. Blend in the ice water, 3 to 4 tablespoons at a time, until the dry ingredients are moistened and the dough holds together. Form the dough into a ball and cut in half. Flatten each half, wrap each half in plastic, and chill in the refrigerator for at least 1 hour.

Strawberry-rhubarb pie

This a combination of sweet and tart using these two seasonal flavors. Instead of doing a whole crust, I like to weave a lattice top, so the fruit will show. Be careful not to overcook the rhubarb because it will get mushy.

Double crust pie shell (see
   recipe, p. 37)

Filling
1 cup sugar
1/4 cup cornstarch
1/2 teaspoon ground cinnamon
Pinch salt
3 cups trimmed (1 1/2 pounds
   untrimmed) rhubarb, cut into
   1/2-inch-thick slices
1 (16-ounce) container strawberries,
   hulled and halved

Glaze
1 large egg yolk, beaten
2 teaspoons water

Prepare the double crust pie shell pastry and refrigerate. Once the dough has chilled, roll out 1 dough ball on a lightly floured surface to a 1/8-inch thickness and transfer to a 9-inch pie pan. Trim the edges, leaving a 3/4-inch overhang. Use a pastry crimper to decorate the crust, if desired. Roll out the second dough ball to a 13-inch round. Cut the dough round into 5 (1 1/2-inch-wide) strips.

Preheat the oven to 400 degrees F.

To make the filling, combine the sugar, cornstarch, cinnamon, and salt in a bowl. Pour the flour mixture over the strawberries and rhubarb in a large bowl and toss gently to combine.

Pour the filling into the prepared pie shell. Arrange 3 of the dough strips atop the filling, spacing them evenly. Form a lattice by placing the remaining 2 strips over the filling in the opposite direction. Trim the ends of the dough strips to be even with the inside of the bottom pie shell.

(continued on page 40)

To make the glaze, combine the beaten egg yolk with the water. Brush the glaze over the pie crust and transfer the pie to a baking sheet. Bake for 20 minutes, then reduce the oven temperature to 350 degrees F. Continue to bake another 35 to 45 minutes, or until the crust becomes golden brown and the filling has thickened.

Transfer the pie to a wire rack and cool completely before serving.

Chocolate buttermilk pie

Serves 8

1 pie shell (see recipe, p. 36)

Filling
2 cups sugar
2 tablespoons all-purpose flour
2 tablespoons cocoa powder
1/2 teaspoon salt
8 tablespoons (1 stick) butter
3 eggs
1 cup buttermilk
2 teaspoons vanilla extract

Preheat the oven to 350 degrees F.

In a small bowl mix the sugar, flour, cocoa powder, and salt. Cream the butter in a mixing bowl, then gradually add the sugar mixture and mix until smooth. Add the eggs and mix well. Stir in the buttermilk and vanilla.

Pour the filling into an unbaked pie shell. Bake 45 to 50 minutes, or until the center is set. Allow the pie to cool completely before serving.

Sweet potato custard pie

Serves 8

1 pie shell (see recipe, p. 36)

Filling
1 pound sweet potatoes
1 cup sugar
1 teaspoon fresh ground nutmeg
3 eggs
8 tablespoons (1 stick) butter,

melted
1 1/2 cups half and half
1 teaspoon vanilla extract
1/2 teaspoon pure lemon extract

Preheat the oven to 350 degrees F.

To make the filling, boil the sweet potatoes for 40 to 50 minutes, or until tender. Drain the potatoes, run them under cold water, and remove the skin. Mash the potatoes in a mixing bowl and stir until smooth, then gradually stir in the sugar and nutmeg. Add the eggs one at a time, then the melted butter and half and half. Finally, stir in the vanilla and lemon extracts.

Pour the filling into the unbaked pie shell. Bake for 45 to 55 minutes, or until a knife inserted in the center comes out clean.

Lemon ice box pie

Serves 8

1 pie shell, prebaked (see recipe,
   p. 36)

Filling
1 (14-ounce) can sweetened
   condensed milk
4 large egg yolks
1/2 cup fresh squeezed lemon juice

Homemade Whipped Cream
1 cup whipping cream
1/2 cup powdered sugar

Garnish (optional)
Lemon slices and zest

Prepare and prebake the pie shell.

To make the filling, whisk together the sweetened condensed milk, egg yolks, and lemon juice in a medium mixing bowl until smooth.

Pour the mixture into the prebaked pie crust. Smooth the filling using a plastic spatula and forming the filling into a slight dome in the center. Bake the pie at 350 degrees F for 15 minutes. Remove the pie from the oven and allow it to cool completely. Wrap in plastic wrap and refrigerate, uncovered, for at least 4 hours, or until set.

To make the whipped cream, beat the whipping cream until it becomes foamy. Gradually add in the powdered sugar, beating until soft peaks form.

Garnish the pie with Homemade Whipped Cream, lemon slices, and zest. Refrigerate 1 hour before serving.

Chocolate mud pie

Serves 8

1 chocolate pie shell (see recipe, p.36)

Filling
8 tablespoons (1 stick) butter,
  softened
1 cup sugar
1/2 cup flour
1/4 teaspoon salt

2 eggs
2 ounces bittersweet chocolate,
  melted
1 teaspoon vanilla extract

Garnish
Homemade Whipped Cream (see
  recipe, p. 45)

Preheat the oven to 350 degrees F.

To make the filling, cream the butter in a mixing bowl.

In a separate bowl combine the sugar, flour, and salt, and add this mixture to the creamed butter. Add the eggs in one at a time. Stir in the melted chocolate and vanilla.

Spoon the filling into the unbaked pie shell. Bake for 30 minutes, or until a knife inserted in the center comes out clean.

Serve with Homemade Whipped Cream.

Apple cider pie

An apple cider reduction is the secret to making this pie more flavorful—it has a mega-apple flavor.

Double crust shell (see
recipe, p. 37)

Filling
2 cups apple cider
6 cups (about 8 whole) apples,
peeled, cored, and sliced
1 tablespoon lemon juice, fresh
squeezed
2/3 cup granulated sugar

2 tablespoons flour
1/2 teaspoon ground cinnamon

Topping
2 tablespoons (1/4 stick) butter,
melted
1 tablespoon sugar

Prepare the double crust pastry according to the recipe. Once the dough is chilled, roll out one of the balls on a lightly floured surface to fit a 9-inch pie pan. Transfer the dough to the pie pan and trim the edges, leaving a 1/2-inch over-hang. Roll the second dough ball to a 1/8-inch thickness.

To prepare the filling, bring the apple cider to a boil in a large, heavy saucepan over high heat. Cook for 45 minutes, or until the liquid has reduced to 1 cup. Allow the apple cider reduction to cool completely.

While the apple cider is boiling, combine the apples and lemon juice in a large mixing bowl.

In a separate bowl, mix the sugar, flour, and cinnamon until well combined. Spoon the cinnamon mixture over the apples and toss gently.

Preheat the oven to 375 degrees F.

Spoon the apple mixture into the bottom of the pie shell and pour the cooled apple cider over the mixture. Place the second half of the pastry dough over the filling and crimp the edges to close. Cut slits in the top of the shell to allow steam to escape while baking. Brush the top with the melted butter and sprinkle with sugar. Bake for 45 to 55 minutes, or until golden brown. Cool on a wire rack before serving.

Chocolate mocha pie

Serves 8

1 pie shell, prebaked (see recipe, p. 36)

Filling
1 cup sugar
1/2 cup all-purpose flour
2 cups milk
2 teaspoons instant coffee
2 (1-ounce) squares unsweetened
   chocolate, finely chopped
3 egg yolks

2 tablespoons (1/4 stick) butter
1 teaspoon vanilla extract

Whipped Cream Topping
2 cups whipping cream
1 teaspoon instant coffee

Garnish
Shaved chocolate

Combine the sugar, flour, milk, instant coffee, and chocolate in a 2-quart saucepan. Stirring constantly, cook over medium heat until the mixture begins to bubble. Continue stirring until the chocolate melts and the mixture is smooth.

Mix a little of the hot chocolate mixture into the egg yolks, beating rapidly to avoid cooking the yolks. Stir the warm yolk mixture into the remainder of the chocolate mixture and cook for an additional 2 to 3 minutes. Remove the mixture from the heat and stir in the butter and vanilla. Pour the filling into the prebaked pie shell and chill until the filling is set.

To make the whipped cream topping, combine the whipping cream and instant coffee and mix until blended. Whip the cream mixture until stiff peaks form. Spoon the whipped cream over the top of the pie and chill until ready to serve.

Garnish the pie with shaved chocolate.

Lemon meringue pie

1 pie shell, prebaked (see recipe, p. 36)

Filling
1 cup sugar
5 tablespoons cornstarch
¼ teaspoon salt
2 cups milk
4 eggs, separated
2 tablespoons unsalted butter

½ cup fresh lemon juice
2 teaspoons lemon zest

Topping
Meringue
4 egg whites
½ teaspoon cream of tartar
Pinch salt
¼ cup sugar

Combine the sugar, cornstarch, and salt in a saucepan and gradually add in the milk. Mix until the cornstarch is dissolved completely. Cook the mixture over moderate heat until it comes to a boil, stirring constantly.

In a mixing bowl, beat the egg yolks. Gradually mix 1 cup of the milk mixture into the egg yolks, then add the yolk mixture into the remaining milk. Simmer over moderate heat for about 3 minutes, stirring constantly. Remove the pan from the heat and stir in the butter, lemon juice, and lemon zest until the butter melts. Set aside and allow the mixture to cool.

Preheat the oven to 350 degrees F.

To make the meringue, beat the egg whites with cream of tartar and salt until they form soft peaks. Gradually beat in the sugar just until the meringue holds stiff peaks.

Pour the filling into the pie shell and spread the meringue over the top, covering completely and sealing the meringue to the shell. Draw the meringue up into peaks using a plastic spatula. Bake the pie in the middle of the oven for 12 to 15 minutes, or until the meringue has golden peaks. Refrigerate until ready to serve.

Old-fashioned buttermilk poundcake

Serves 12 to 16

The buttermilk in this recipe adds a moist texture to the poundcake. Buttermilk is a Southern staple, so you'll see it in quite a few desserts in this book.

8 tablespoons (1 stick) butter
1 cup shortening
2 cups sugar
4 eggs
1 tablespoon vanilla extract
3 cups all-purpose flour

1/4 teaspoon salt
1/2 teaspoon baking soda
1 cup buttermilk

Preheat the oven to 325 degrees F. Grease and flour a 10-inch tube pan.

In a mixing bowl, cream together the butter, shortening, and sugar until light and fluffy. Add the eggs one at a time, beating well after each addition. Blend in the vanilla. In a separate bowl, sift together the flour, salt, and baking soda. Alternately add the flour mixture and the buttermilk to the creamed mixture, beginning and ending with the flour mixture. Mix well after each addition.

Spoon the batter into the prepared pan. Bake for 75 minutes, or until a toothpick inserted 1 inch from the edge comes out clean. Allow the poundcake to cool in the pan for 10 minutes, then turn out onto a wire rack or floured board to cool completely before serving.

7Up poundcake

Serves 12 to 16

Poundcake
1 cup (2 sticks) butter
1/2 cup shortening
3 cups sugar
5 large eggs
3 cups flour
3/4 cup 7Up

Glaze
1 1/2 cups powdered sugar
Zest of 1 lemon
3 to 4 tablespoons lemon juice,
  fresh squeezed

Preheat the oven to 325 degrees F.

Grease and flour a 10-inch tube pan, or spray it with nonstick cooking spray.

Cream together the butter and shortening. Gradually add the sugar and beat until the mixture is light and fluffy. Add the eggs one at a time and beat well. Using a mixer at low speed, gradually add the flour. Add the 7Up and mix until just combined.

Pour the batter into the prepared pan and bake for 1 1/2 hours, or until a toothpick inserted in the center comes out clean. Allow the poundcake to cool in the pan for 10 minutes, then turn out onto a serving dish.

To make the glaze, combine the powdered sugar and zest in a small mixing bowl. Add the juice and stir until the mixture is smooth.

Poke holes in the top of the poundcake with a skewer, and drizzle with the glaze before serving.

Cream cheese poundcake

My mother recently reminded me that she made this poundcake when I was little every time I had to bring a dessert to school to share with the class or for a special school event.

1 1/2 cups (3 sticks) butter

1 (8-ounce) package cream cheese

3 cups sugar

6 eggs

2 teaspoons pure lemon extract

2 teaspoons pure vanilla extract

3 cups unbleached all-purpose flour, sifted

Grease and flour a 10-inch tube pan.

Using a mixer, cream together the butter, cream cheese, and sugar until the mixture is light and fluffy. Add the eggs one at a time, beating well after each addition. Stir in the lemon and vanilla extracts. With the mixer set on low speed, gradually add the sifted flour until the mixture is smooth. Beat until just combined.

Pour the batter into the prepared pan. Place the pan in a cold oven and bake at 325 degrees F for 1 1/2 hours, or until a toothpick inserted in the center comes out clean. Remove from the oven and allow the cake to cool in the pan for 10 minutes before turning out onto a wire rack. Cool completely before serving.

Chocolate buttermilk poundcake

Serves 12 to 16

Poundcake
1 cup shortening
2 cups sugar
4 eggs
1 (4-ounce) bar sweet baking
    chocolate, melted and cooled
3 cups all-purpose flour
1/2 teaspoon baking soda
1/2 teaspoon salt

1 cup buttermilk
2 teaspoons vanilla extract
1/2 teaspoon orange extract

Chocolate Glaze (see recipe, p. 189)

Garnish
Powdered sugar
Fresh strawberries

Grease and flour a 10-inch tube pan.

Cream the shortening and gradually add the sugar, beating until the mixture is light and fluffy. Add the eggs one at a time, beating after each addition. Stir in the chocolate and mix well.

In a separate bowl, combine the flour, baking soda, and salt and mix well. Alternately add the flour mixture and the buttermilk to the creamed mixture, beginning and ending with the flour mixture. After each addition, mix until just blended. Add the extracts, mixing until just blended.

Pour the batter into the prepared pan. Bake at 350 degrees F for 1 1/2 hours. Allow the poundcake to cool in the pan for 10 to 15 minutes, then invert the cake onto a serving plate.

Spoon Chocolate Glaze over the top of the warm cake and cool completely before serving.

Garnish with a sprinkling of powdered sugar and serve with fresh strawberries.

Sweet potato poundcake with molasses glaze

Poundcake
2 cups (1 pound) sweet potatoes
3 cups all-purpose flour
2 teaspoons baking powder
1/2 teaspoon baking soda
1/2 teaspoon fresh ground nutmeg
1/2 teaspoon salt
2 sticks unsalted butter
2 cups sugar
4 large eggs
1 teaspoon vanilla extract

Molasses Glaze
1 cup powdered sugar, sifted
2 tablespoons molasses
1/4 teaspoon fresh ground nutmeg

Bake the sweet potatoes at 375 degrees F for 1 hour, or until tender. Allow the potatoes to cool, then peel, mash, and set aside in a bowl.

Preheat the oven to 350 degrees F. Thoroughly grease and flour a 10-inch tube pan, or spray it with baking spray.

In a medium bowl mix together the flour, baking powder, baking soda, nutmeg, and salt; set aside. In a large mixing bowl, cream the butter and sugar until light and fluffy, stopping once or twice to scrape down the sides of the bowl. Add the eggs one at a time, beating well after each addition. Add the vanilla and sweet potatoes, and mix until the batter is combined. (Expect that the batter may look curdled at this point.)

With the mixer on low speed gradually add in the flour mixture. Mix to just incorporate.

Scrape the batter into the prepared pan and bake for 45 to 50 minutes, or until the cake springs back when pressed lightly and a toothpick inserted in the center comes out clean.

Cool the cake in the pan on a wire rack for 20 minutes. Run a thin knife around the edge to loosen the cake, and then carefully invert it onto the rack to cool completely.

To make the glaze, combine the powdered sugar, molasses, and nutmeg in a small bowl. Mix until the sugar is completely absorbed and the glaze is smooth. Spoon the glaze over the cake while it is still warm and serve.

Fresh apple poundcake

Serves 12 to 16

1 cup vegetable oil
1 1/2 cups sugar
3 eggs
1 teaspoon vanilla extract
3 cups unbleached all-purpose flour
1 teaspoon ground cinnamon
1/2 teaspoon salt
1 teaspoon baking soda

2 cups (1 or 2 large, whole) apples,
  peeled and chopped
2 cups pecans, chopped

Preheat the oven to 350 degrees F. Grease and flour a 10-inch tube pan.

In a medium bowl, combine the oil and sugar. Beat in the eggs one at a time, mixing well after each addition. Stir in the vanilla.

In a separate bowl combine the flour, cinnamon, salt, and baking soda. Stir the flour mixture into the egg mixture. Fold in the apples and nuts and pour the batter into the prepared pan.

Bake for 1 1/2 hours, or until a toothpick inserted in the center comes out clean. Allow the cake to cool in the pan for 10 minutes before transferring it to a serving plate.

Drizzle the warm cake with Divine Caramel Sauce (see recipe, p. 197) before serving.

Brown sugar poundcake

Serves 12 to 16

1 cup (2 sticks) butter, softened
1/2 cup shortening
2 cups brown sugar, firmly packed
1 cup granulated sugar
6 large eggs
3 cups unbleached all-purpose flour
1/2 teaspoon salt

1 teaspoon baking powder
1 cup evaporated milk
2 teaspoons vanilla extract

Grease and flour a 10-inch tube pan.

In a mixer, beat together the butter and shortening on medium speed until creamy. Gradually add the sugars and beat until light and fluffy. Add the eggs one at a time and mix well.

In a separate bowl, combine the flour, salt, and baking powder. Alternately add the flour mixture and the milk to the butter mixture, beginning and ending with the flour mixture. Mix the batter at low speed after each addition until just blended. Stir in the vanilla.

Pour the batter into the prepared pan. Place the pan in a cold oven and set the oven temperature to 350 degrees F. Bake for 1 1/2 to 1 3/4 hours, or until a toothpick inserted in the center of the cake comes out clean. Allow the cake to cool in the pan for 10 to 15 minutes. Transfer from the pan to a wire rack and cool completely before serving.

Sour cream poundcake with lemon glaze

Serves 12 to 16

Poundcake
1 cup (2 sticks) butter
3 cups sugar
6 large eggs
3 cups all-purpose flour
Pinch salt
1/4 teaspoon baking soda
1 cup sour cream
2 teaspoons lemon extract
1/2 teaspoon vanilla extract

Lemon Glaze
1 cup powdered sugar
2 tablespoons fresh squeezed
   lemon juice
1 teaspoon lemon zest

Preheat the oven to 325 degrees F. Grease and flour a 10-inch tube pan.

In a mixing bowl cream together the butter and sugar until light and fluffy. Add the eggs one at a time and beat at low speed with a mixer for 1 minute, stopping to scrape the sides of the bowl. Increase the speed to medium and beat for 2 minutes.

In a separate bowl, mix the flour, salt, and baking soda.

In another bowl, mix the sour cream and extracts. Alternately add the flour and the sour cream mixtures to the batter until both are fully incorporated.

Pour the batter into the prepared pan and bake for 1 1/2 hours, or until a toothpick inserted in the center comes out clean. Allow the cake to cool in the pan on a wire rack for 10 minutes before transferring the cake to the rack to cool completely.

To make the glaze, combine the powdered sugar, lemon juice, and zest in a bowl and beat until smooth. While the cake is still warm, poke holes into the surface with a skewer and drizzle the lemon glaze evenly over the cake.

Rich's rum poundcake

♡

This is the one of the few desserts my mother would purchase from the store—Rich's Department Store, hence the name. I was inspired to create a recipe of my own that echoed this memorable childhood treat.

Poundcake
1 cup (2 sticks) butter
2 1/2 cups granulated sugar
6 eggs
2 teaspoons vanilla extract
3 cups unbleached all-purpose flour
1/4 teaspoon baking soda
1 cup sour cream

Garnish
Buttered Rum Sauce (see recipe,
   p. 192)
1/2 cup walnuts, chopped

Preheat the oven to 350 degrees F. Grease and flour a 10-inch tube pan.

Cream the butter in a mixing bowl. Gradually add the granulated sugar, beating until the mixture is light and fluffy. Add the eggs one at a time, beating well after each addition. Beat in the vanilla.

In a separate bowl, combine the flour and baking soda and add this into the batter in three parts, alternating with the sour cream, and beginning and ending with the flour mixture. Mix just until blended.

Spoon the batter into the prepared pan and bake for 75 minutes. Allow the cake to cool in the pan for 15 minutes, then remove the cake from the pan and place on a serving plate. Punch holes in the top of cake with a skewer. Drizzle the cake evenly with Buttered Rum Sauce and sprinkle with chopped walnuts.

Old-fashioned pork cake

Serves 12 to 16

Pork in a poundcake? I discovered this in an old cookbook, so I started serving it on special occasions. It has been really well received—Southerners really do love pork! You can add canned fruit to the recipe for variety.

1 pound fresh pork sausage
3 cups brown sugar, firmly packed
1 egg, lightly beaten
1 teaspoon baking soda
1 cup strong coffee, cold
1 cup raisins
1 cup walnuts or pecans

1 teaspoon salt
1 teaspoon cinnamon
1 teaspoon fresh ground nutmeg
1 teaspoon allspice

Preheat the oven to 350 degrees F. Grease a 9- or 10-inch tube pan and line the bottom with wax paper.

Mix together the sausage and the sugar. Add the beaten egg and mix well.

In a separate bowl mix the baking soda and coffee, then stir this mixture into the sausage. Add the raisins, nuts, salt, and spices and mix well. The batter will be very stiff.

Turn the batter into the prepared tube pan and bake for 1 hour or until the cake shrinks from the sides of the pan and a toothpick inserted in the center comes out clean. Cool for 10 minutes in the pan before turning out onto a wire rack to cool completely.

Serve with Apple Jelly (see recipe, p. 182).

Old-fashioned poundcake with brandied apricot glaze

Serves 12 to 16

Poundcake
2 cups (4 sticks) butter
3 cups sugar
6 eggs
4 cups all-purpose flour
1 cup half and half
1 tablespoon pure vanilla extract
1 tablespoon pure lemon extract

Brandied Apricot Glaze
10 ounces Apricot Jam (see recipe, p. 177)
1 teaspoon ginger, freshly grated
3 ounces brandy

Spray a 10-inch tube pan and dust lightly with flour. Set aside.

Cream together the butter and sugar at medium speed. Add the eggs one at a time, beating well after each addition. Scrape the sides of the bowl often. Reduce the mixer speed to low and add the flour alternately with the half and half, starting and ending with the flour. Add the vanilla and lemon extracts. Scrape the bowl again to ensure even blending, and spoon the batter into the prepared tube pan. Give the pan a sharp rap on the counter to dislodge any air bubbles.

Place the cake in a cold oven and bake at 350 degrees F for 1 1/2 hours, or until a toothpick inserted in the center comes out clean. The cake will rise slightly above the pan. Remove the cake from the oven and let cool in the pan for 15 minutes before transferring to a wire rack.

While the cake is baking, cook the Apricot Jam in a saucepan over medium heat until it melts. Remove from the heat, add the ginger and allow the mixture to cool slightly. Add the brandy and let the glaze cool to room temperature. Pour the glaze over the warm cake, allowing it to drip down the sides, and serve.

Classic southern chocolate poundcake

Serves 12 to 16

1 pound unsalted butter, softened
3 cups sugar
5 eggs
3 cups unbleached all-purpose flour
1/2 cup unsweetened natural
   cocoa powder
1/2 teaspoon baking powder

1/2 teaspoon salt
1/2 cup milk
1/2 cup strong coffee
1 tablespoon vanilla extract

Preheat the oven to 325 degrees F. Grease and flour a 10-inch tube pan.

In a mixing bowl, beat the butter with an electric mixer at medium speed until creamy. Gradually add the sugar and beat until light and creamy. Add the eggs one at a time, beating just until blended.

In a separate bowl combine the flour, cocoa powder, baking powder, and salt and set aside.

In another small bowl, combine the milk and the coffee and set aside.

With the mixer on low speed, alternately add the flour mixture and the milk to the butter mixture, beginning and ending with the flour. Beat until just blended. Add the vanilla and stir to combine.

Pour the batter into the prepared pan. Bake for 1 1/2 hours, or until a toothpick inserted in the center comes out clean. Allow the cake to cool in the pan for 10 minutes before transferring to a wire rack to cool completely.

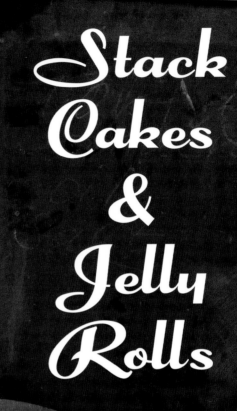

Stack Cakes & Jelly Rolls

♡ # Dried apple stack cake

Yields 1 (7-layer) cake

Cake
5 1/2 cups unbleached all-purpose
   flour
1 teaspoon salt
1 teaspoon baking powder
1 teaspoon baking soda
1 teaspoon ground cinnamon
1 cup (2 sticks) unsalted butter,
   softened
2 1/2 cups light brown sugar,
   firmly packed
2 eggs
1 tablespoon vanilla extract
1/2 cup buttermilk

Spiced Apple Filling
1 pound dried apples
5 cups water
2 cups light brown sugar, firmly
   packed
2 teaspoons fresh ground nutmeg
2 teaspoons ground cinnamon
1/2 teaspoon ground cloves
Pinch salt

Garnish
Divine Caramel Sauce (see recipe,
   p. 197)
1 cup chopped walnuts

Preheat the oven to 425 degrees F. Grease and flour 7 (9-inch) cake pans and set aside.

In a large bowl combine the flour, salt, baking powder, baking soda, and cinnamon.

In a separate mixing bowl beat the butter at medium speed until creamy. Gradually add in the sugar, and continue to beat for 2 to 3 minutes. Add the eggs one at a time, beating well after each addition. Stir in the vanilla. Alternately add the flour mixture and the buttermilk to the butter mixture, beating at a low speed after each addition until just combined. The dough will be stiff.

Divide the dough evenly among the prepared pans, placing approximately 3/4 cup dough into each pan. With floured hands, press the dough into the pans evenly. Bake the cakes for 10 minutes or until a golden crust forms. Remove from the oven and turn the layers out onto a wire rack to cool completely. Each cake layer will be 1/4- to 3/8-inch thick.

To make the spiced apple filling, pulse the dried apples in a food processor until coarsely chopped. Bring the water to boil in a large stockpot over medium-high heat. Add the apples to the boiling water, reduce the heat to medium and cook uncovered, stirring frequently, for 20 to 30 minutes or until all the water is absorbed. Add the sugar, nutmeg, cinnamon, cloves, and salt and simmer for 15 more minutes, stirring frequently.

To assemble the cake stack, spread each layer with approximately 3/4 cup hot apple filling. Top the cake with the remaining apple filling. Wrap with plastic or place on a cake stand with a cover. Allow the cake to stand for at least 24 hours before serving.

When ready to serve, drizzle the cake with Divine Caramel Sauce, letting the sauce drip down the sides. Garnish with chopped walnuts.

Peach butter stack cake ♡

Cake
1 cup sugar
1 cup shortening
1 cup sorghum molasses
1 egg
1/4 cup buttermilk
1 teaspoon vanilla extract
2 teaspoons baking soda
1 tablespoon vinegar

1/2 teaspoon salt
1 teaspoon fresh ground nutmeg
1/2 teaspoon ginger
5 cups flour

Filling
Peach Butter Filling (see recipe,
  p. 178)

Preheat the oven to 350 degrees F. Grease and flour 7 (8-inch) cake pans.

Cream together the sugar, shortening, and molasses. Add the egg, buttermilk, and vanilla and mix well. Add the baking soda, vinegar, salt, nutmeg, and ginger. Stir in the flour and mix well.

Divide the dough into 6 uniform balls—the batter will be stiff. Using your fingers, press each ball of dough evenly into a cake pan. The batter will be thin in the pan. Bake for 15 minutes or until lightly browned. Each cake layer will be 1/4- to 3/8-inch thick.

Remove the cakes from the pans while they are still warm and allow them to cool. Once the cakes are cool, spread Peach Butter between each layer of the cake, and top the cake with the remaining butter. The assembled cake will resemble a stack of pancakes.

Strawberry jam stack cake

Yields 1 (7-layer) cake

What I love about stack cakes is that they are so commanding and grand. Traditionally, the bigger the stack cake and the more layers it has, the more important the occasion.

Cake 8 tablespoons (1 stick) unsalted
  butter
1 ounce shortening
1 1/4 cups sugar
3 eggs
1 teaspoon vanilla extract
3 cups cake flour

1/2 teaspoon salt
1 teaspoon baking soda
2 1/2 teaspoons baking powder
1 cup milk

Filling
1 recipe Strawberry Jam (see
  recipe, p. 179)

Preheat the oven to 400 degrees F. Grease 7 (8-inch) round cake pans and line with parchment or wax paper.

In a mixer, cream together the butter, shortening, and sugar until fluffy. With the mixer on medium speed, beat in the eggs one at a time until the eggs are fully incorporated. Stir in the vanilla.

In a separate bowl, combine the flour, salt, baking soda, and baking powder. With the mixer on low, alternately add the flour mixture and the milk to the butter mixture, starting and ending with the flour. Beat on medium speed for 2 to 3 minutes, scraping down the sides of the bowl.

Spread 3/4 cup of the batter into each pan. Bake for 6 to 8 minutes, or until the cake springs back when lightly touched. Turn the cakes out of the pans onto a wire rack while still warm. Repeat until all 7 layers are baked. Each cake layer will be 1/4- to 3/8-inch thick.

Place the first layer on a cake stand and spread 1/2 cup Strawberry Jam over the top. Place the second layer on top of the jam and spread another 1/2 cup jam over the top. Repeat this process until all 7 layers are stacked and layered with jam. Wrap the cake with plastic wrap or foil and allow it to stand for 24 hours before serving.

Blueberry jam jelly roll

Although jelly rolls are an old dessert that we don't see very often today, they are worthy of being brought back into the spotlight. These cakes are a great way to use the jams and jellies that you already have in your cupboard, if you don't have the time to make your own.

Cake
1/4 teaspoon baking powder
1/4 teaspoon salt
4 eggs
3/4 cup sugar, sifted
3/4 cup cake flour
1 teaspoon lemon extract

2 tablespoons powdered sugar,
    for dusting towel, plus more for
    garnish

Filling
1 cup Blueberry Jam (see recipe, p. 186)

Line the bottom of a 15 x 10 x 1-inch jelly roll pan with parchment paper.

Combine the baking powder, salt, and eggs in a bowl. Beat with an electric mixer until the batter is thick and lemon-colored. Fold in the flour and lemon extract.

Spread the batter into the prepared pan and bake at 400 degrees F for 13 minutes, or until the dough springs back when lightly touched. Remove from the oven and quickly trim the crisp edges of the cake.

Dust a towel or cloth with the powdered sugar and turn the cake out onto the towel. Peel off the parchment paper. Quickly spread the Blueberry Jam onto the cake and roll the cake up. Wrap the jelly roll in the cloth and cool on a wire rack. To serve, transfer to a serving dish, seam side down, and dust with powdered sugar.

♡ Chocolate orange marmalade jelly cake

This is a recipe I found in What Mrs. Fisher Knows About Old Southern Cooking *and updated. She has several recipes for jams, jellies, and jelly cakes in her book, and this inspired me to put a chocolate twist on a classic Southern favorite.*

Cake
1 cup sugar
1 cup shortening
1 cup molasses
1 egg
1/2 cup buttermilk
2 teaspoons baking soda
1 tablespoon vinegar

1/2 teaspoon salt
1 teaspoon vanilla extract
5 cups flour
1/2 cup cocoa powder

Filling
1 recipe Orange Marmalade (see
   recipe, p. 181)

Preheat the oven to 350 degrees F. Grease and flour 7 (8-inch) cake pans.

Cream together the sugar and shortening. Gradually stir in the molasses. Add the egg and buttermilk and mix well. Add in the baking soda, vinegar, salt, and vanilla. Stir in the flour and cocoa and mix well.

Divide the dough into 7 uniform balls—the batter will be stiff. Using your fingers, press each ball of dough evenly into a cake pan. The batter will be thin in the pan. Bake for 12 to 15 minutes or until lightly browned. Each cake layer will be 1/4- to 3/8-inch thick.

Remove the cakes from the pans while they are still warm and set aside to cool. Once cooled, spread each with Orange Marmalade as you stack them, reserving some marmalade to spread on the top of the cake.

Blackberry jam with black walnut jelly roll

Serves 8 to 10

Cake
1/2 cup flour
1 teaspoon baking powder
Pinch salt
1/2 teaspoon cinnamon
4 eggs
1/2 cup sugar
1 teaspoon hot water
1 teaspoon vanilla extract

Filling
1 cup black walnuts
1 cup Blackberry Jam (see recipe, p.172)
2 tablespoons powdered sugar, for dusting towel

Garnish
Fresh blackberries
Chopped walnuts

Line the bottom of a 15 x 10 x 1-inch jelly roll pan with parchment paper.

Combine the flour, baking powder, salt, and cinnamon and set aside.

Using a mixer, beat the eggs at high speed until foamy.

In a separate bowl, gradually add the sugar to the eggs and beat until the mixture becomes thick and lemon-colored. Add the water and vanilla. Fold in the flour mixture.

Spread the batter in the jelly roll pan and bake at 375 degrees F for 10 to 17 minutes. Remove from the oven and immediately remove the cake from the pan. Use a knife to trim the crust off the edges.

Spread the powdered sugar over a towel or cloth and turn the cake out onto the towel. Peel off the parchment paper.

Spread the cake with the Blackberry Jam. Sprinkle the walnuts over the jam and roll the cake in the towel. Cool on a wire rack. To serve, place the jelly roll on a serving dish, seam side down.

Garnish with fresh blackberries and walnuts to serve.

Double chocolate jelly roll

Serves 8 to 10

Cake

5 eggs, separated
1 cup sugar, divided
1 teaspoon hot water
1/4 cup flour
1 teaspoon baking powder
4 tablespoons cocoa powder, sifted
2 tablespoons powdered sugar, for
   dusting a towel

Chocolate Frosting Filling

4 (1-ounce) unsweetened chocolate
   squares
4 tablespoons (1/2 stick) butter
1/2 cup milk
1/8 teaspoon salt
3 cups powdered sugar
1 teaspoon vanilla extract

Line the bottom of a 15 x 10 x 1-inch jelly roll pan with parchment paper.

Beat the egg yolks until they are thick and lemon-colored. Gradually add in 1/2 cup sugar, beating continually. Stir in the hot water. In a separate bowl beat the egg whites until foamy and gradually add in the remaining sugar, beating until stiff peaks form. Fold the yolk mixture into the whites.

In a separate bowl, combine the flour, baking powder, and cocoa and fold into the egg mixture.

Spread the batter evenly in the prepared pan. Bake at 400 degrees F for 12 to 15 minutes, or until the cake springs back when gently touched. Remove from the oven and immediately loosen the cake from the sides of the pan.

Dust a towel or cloth with the powdered sugar and turn the cake out onto the towel. Peel off the parchment paper. Starting at the narrow end, roll the cake up in the towel. Cool on a wire rack with the seam side down.

To make the chocolate frosting filling, combine the chocolate, butter, milk, and salt in a saucepan over medium heat. Stir constantly until the chocolate and butter are melted. Remove from the heat, add the powdered sugar and vanilla, and stir until smooth.

Unroll the cake and remove from the towel. Spread the cake with the chocolate frosting filling and re-roll. Place the jelly roll on a serving dish, seam side down.

Damson plum sugar 'n spice jelly roll

Serves 8 to 10

Cake
3 eggs, separated
1 teaspoon vegetable oil
1 teaspoon vanilla extract
1 cup sugar, divided
1/2 cup flour
1 teaspoon baking powder
1/4 teaspoon salt

1/4 teaspoon cinnamon
1/4 teaspoon cloves
2 tablespoons powdered sugar, for dusting towel

Filling
1 1/2 cups Damson Plum Preserves
  (see recipe, p. 175)

Line a 15 x 10 x 1-inch jelly roll pan with parchment paper.

Beat the egg yolks at high speed until they become thick and lemon-colored. Gradually add in the oil, vanilla, and 1/2 cup sugar.

In a separate bowl, beat the egg whites until foamy and gradually add in the remaining sugar, beating until stiff peaks form. Fold the egg whites into the yolk mixture.

Combine the flour, baking powder, salt, cinnamon, and cloves in a small mixing bowl. Fold into the egg mixture.

Spread the dough into the prepared pan and bake at 350 degrees for 10 to 12 minutes or until the dough springs back when touched.

Dust a towel or cloth with the powdered sugar and turn the cake out onto the towel. Peel the parchment off the bottom of the cake.

Spread 1 cup of Damson Plum Presesrves over the cake. Roll the cake in the towel and allow it to cool, seam side down. To serve, transfer the jelly roll to a serving dish, seam side down. Spread the remaining 1/2 cup of Damson Plum Preserves over the top and sides and serve.

Chocolate jelly roll with coconut-pecan filling

Cake

1 teaspoon baking powder

1/8 teaspoon salt

4 eggs

1 cup sugar, sifted

1/2 cup flour

3 tablespoons cocoa powder, plus
more for dusting

1 teaspoon vanilla extract

2 tablespoons powdered sugar, for
dusting towel

Filling

1/2 recipe Coconut-Pecan Filling
(see German Chocolate Cake
recipe, p.121)

Line a 15 x 10 x 1-inch jelly roll pan with parchment paper.

In a mixing bowl, beat the baking powder, salt, eggs, and sugar until it forms a thick, lemon-colored batter.

In a separate bowl, combine the flour and cocoa and fold into the egg mixture. Stir in the vanilla.

Spread the batter in a jelly roll pan and bake at 400 degrees F for 12 minutes, or until the center of the dough springs back when touched. Remove from the oven and trim the crust from the edges.

Dust a towel or cloth with the powdered sugar and turn the cake out onto the towel. Peel off the parchment paper. Spread the coconut-pecan filling on one side of the cake, roll the cake, and cover it with the towel. Place on a wire rack, seam side down, and allow it to cool.

Remove the cloth and transfer the roll to a serving plate, seam side down. Dust the roll with cocoa and slice diagonally to serve.

Puddings
&
Cobblers

Cinnamon raisin bread pudding

Serves 12 to 15

1 pound white bread, sliced
8 tablespoons (1 stick) butter,
  melted
1 1/2 cups raisins
4 cups milk

3 eggs
2 cups sugar
2 teaspoons vanilla extract
2 teaspoons cinnamon

Preheat the oven to 350 degrees F.

Pour half the melted butter in the bottom of a casserole dish. Line the dish with the slices of white bread. Drizzle the remaining butter over the bread and sprinkle the raisins on top.

In a large mixing bowl, stir the milk, eggs, sugar, vanilla, and cinnamon until well blended. Pour 1/3 of the milk mixture over the bread and let it soak for 10 minutes. Pour another 1/3 of the milk mixture over the bread and let it soak another 10 minutes. Repeat with the remainder of the milk mixture.

Bake for 45 minutes, or until the pudding springs back when lightly touched. Cool and serve with Nutmeg Sauce (see recipe, p.198).

Banana pudding

Pudding
3 tablespoons flour
1 1/2 cups sugar
1/4 teaspoon salt
3 cups milk
4 egg yolks
2 teaspoons vanilla extract
1 (12-ounce) box vanilla wafers
6 large bananas, sliced

Meringue
4 egg whites
1/4 cup sugar

Preheat the oven to 375 degrees F.

In a saucepan combine the flour, sugar, and salt. Stir in the milk and cook over medium heat for 5 minutes.

Beat the egg yolks in a mixing bowl. Slowly add 1/2 cup of the milk mixture to the egg yolks to combine; then add the yolk mixture back into the remaining milk mixture in the saucepan. Cook over medium heat, stirring constantly, for 12 to 15 minutes, or until the mixture is smooth and coats the back of a wooden spoon. Remove from the heat and add the vanilla.

Spread a thin layer of the pudding on the bottom of an oven-safe bowl or baking dish. Layer 1/3 of the wafers over the pudding, then cover the wafers with 1/3 of the banana slices. Pour 1/3 of the custard over the bananas. Continue to alternate layers of the wafers, bananas, and custard, ending with a layer of custard.

To make the meringue, beat the egg whites until foamy. Slowly add 1/4 cup sugar and beat until stiff peaks form. Spread the meringue over the custard and seal the edges. Bake for 10 minutes, or until the peaks of the meringue turn golden brown.

Stirred pudding

Serves 6 to 8

Pudding
3 cups milk
3 eggs
1 cup sugar
2 teaspoons vanilla extract

Garnish
Fresh or macerated seasonal fruit
Chocolate sauce, or your choice
     of toppings

Heat the milk in a saucepan, stirring with a wooden spoon so the bottom doesn't burn.

In a separate bowl, beat the eggs and sugar until the mixture thickens. Slowly add 1/2 cup of the milk to the egg mixture and stir to combine. Add the egg mixture to the milk in the saucepan. Cook over medium heat, stirring constantly, for 20 to 30 minutes or until the pudding thickens. Remove from the heat and stir in the vanilla.

To serve, transfer the pudding into individual serving cups and garnish with fresh or macerated fruit, chocolate sauce, or your topping of choice.

Rhubarb crisps

Filling

1 cup sugar

3 tablespoons all-purpose flour

2 tablespoons (1/4 stick) unsalted
   butter, melted

1/2 teaspoon orange zest

1/2 teaspoon fresh ground nutmeg

6 cups trimmed (about 3 pounds
   untrimmed) rhubarb, cut into
   1/2-inch pieces

Streusel Topping

1 cup light brown sugar

1 cup walnuts, chopped

1/2 cup all-purpose flour

2 tablespoons (1/4 stick) unsalted
   butter, melted

Preheat the oven to 375 degrees F.

In a mixing bowl combine the sugar, flour, butter, zest, and nutmeg. Add the rhubarb pieces and toss gently to combine.

In a separate bowl combine the light brown sugar, walnuts, flour, and butter to make the topping.

Spoon the rhubarb mixture into 6 individual baking cups. Crumble the topping over each cup. Bake for 30 minutes, or until the topping is a golden color and the filling is bubbly.

Serve warm with your favorite vanilla ice cream and a dollop of Homemade Whipped Cream (see recipe, p.45).

Rice pudding

Serves 10 to 12

Adding a layer of strawberry jam lends interest to a dessert that is sometimes thought to be a bit too ordinary to be special. Not! Think stripes—add blueberry jam, too, for a real July 4th treat.

4 cups water	Pinch salt
1 teaspoon salt	3 eggs
2 cups medium grain rice, uncooked	1 teaspoon vanilla extract
6 cups milk	1/4 teaspoon cinnamon
1 cup sugar	

To cook the rice, bring the water and salt to a boil in a saucepan over high heat. Stir in the rice, cover, and reduce the heat. Simmer the rice for 18 minutes, then allow it to cool.

Preheat the oven to 325 degrees F.

Spread the rice in the bottom of a 9 x 13-inch baking dish.

Combine the milk, sugar, and salt in a mixing bowl. Add the eggs one at a time, beating after each addition. Stir in the vanilla and cinnamon.

Pour the milk mixture over the rice and bake for 35 to 45 minutes, or until set. Remove from the oven and allow the pudding to cool before serving.

To serve, layer the rice pudding in a bowl or jar (as shown) with Strawberry Jam (see recipe, p.179), or your choice of jam or jelly.

Apple roly poly

I prepared this recipe alongside Edna Lewis in the cooking sessions we taught. I had never heard of a roly poly before and she taught me how to make it.

Roly poly

2 quarts water, or enough to cover
   the roly poly
1 egg, well beaten
1/2 cup milk
1/2 stick butter, plus 2 ounces,
   melted, for brushing roly poly
1/4 teaspoon salt
1 teaspoon baking powder
4 tablespoons flour, or enough to
   make a stiff dough
1 pound apples, thinly sliced

Cinnamon Sugar

1/4 cup sugar
1 teaspoon cinnamon

Cranberry Sauce

1 cup cream
1 cup sugar
2/3 cup vinegar
1 tablespoon cornstarch
1 cup cranberries

Place a pot of water on the stove and fill with 2 quarts water. Bring to a boil.

While the water is heating, combine the beaten egg, milk, and 1/2 stick butter in a mixing bowl.

In a separate bowl, combine the salt and baking powder. Add the dry ingredients to the egg mixture and mix well. Stir in the flour, 1 tablespoon at a time, using just enough to make the dough stiff.

Once the dough is stiff, roll it out on a lightly floured surface to a 1/2-inch thickness. Form the dough into a rectangle and brush liberally with the melted butter. Sprinkle the cinnamon sugar onto the dough and lay the apple slices over the sugar in rows. Transfer the dough to a cheese cloth and roll the dough tightly into a log. Wrap the cheese cloth tightly around the log, securing both ends and tying with kitchen twine so the log retains its shape as it boils.

Submerge the roly poly in the boiling water and continue to boil for 45 minutes, or until the dough is firm to the touch. Remove the pot of water from the heat and use a spatula to transfer the roly poly to a platter to cool before serving.

To make the cranberry sauce, mix the cream, sugar, vinegar, and cornstarch in a saucepan. Cook over medium-high heat until the sauce thickens. Add the cranberries and cook for 2 minutes more. To serve, pour the sauce over the roly poly, and pass any extra sauce around the table to pour over individual slices.

Fresh peach cobbler

Pastry Dough
2 1/2 cups all-purpose flour
3 tablespoons sugar
1 teaspoon salt
1/2 cup shortening
8 tablespoons (1 stick) unsalted butter
1/2 cup cold water

Filling
3 cups sugar
1 teaspoon fresh ground nutmeg

4 tablespoons flour
1 teaspoon vanilla extract
3 pounds fresh peaches, peeled, pitted and sliced
8 tablespoons (1 stick) butter, cut into pieces

Topping
2 tablespoons sugar
3 tablespoons (3/8 stick) butter, melted

In a medium bowl, sift together the flour, 3 tablespoons sugar, and salt. Using a pastry blender or fork, cut in the shortening and butter until the mixture resembles coarse crumbs. Sprinkle cold water over the flour mixture and work the dough with your hands until it forms a ball. Refrigerate the dough for at least 30 minutes to chill it. Once the dough is chilled, roll the dough out onto a lightly floured surface to a 1/8-inch thickness. Cut the dough into 1-inch-wide strips.

Preheat the oven to 400 degrees F.

To make the filling, combine the sugar, nutmeg, and flour in a large mixing bowl. Add the vanilla and stir the peaches into the flour mixture.

Pour the mixture into a 9 x 13-inch baking dish. Dot the filling with butter.

Weave the strips of dough into a lattice over the peach filling.

To make the topping, drizzle the sugar with the melted melted butter and stir. Sprinkle the dough with the topping. Bake at 400 degrees F for 15 minutes, then reduce the oven temperature to 350 degrees F and bake for another 40 minutes, or until the cobbler turns a golden brown.

Serve with Nutmeg Sauce (see recipe, p.198).

♡ Granny smith apple cobbler

Serves 12 to 15

Filling

4 pounds Granny Smith apples,
  peeled, cored and sliced
1 tablespoon fresh squeezed lemon
  juice
1/4 cup flour
2 teaspoons ground cinnamon
1 1/2 cups sugar
2 tablespoons (1/4 stick) unsalted
  butter, chilled, and cut into
  small pieces

Dough

2 cups all-purpose flour
3 tablespoons sugar
1 tablespoon baking powder
5 tablespoons shortening
3/4 cup milk

Preheat the oven to 400 degrees F. Butter a deep 9 x 13-inch baking dish.

Place the sliced apples in a large bowl and sprinkle them with lemon juice. Mix the flour, cinnamon, and sugar together in a separate bowl. Sprinkle the cinnamon mixture over the apples and toss gently to coat.

In a medium bowl, mix the flour, sugar, and baking powder. Cut in the shortening until the mixture becomes crumbly. Add the milk and stir with a fork. Form the dough into a ball and turn out onto a lightly floured surface. Roll the dough out to a size that is 1/2 to 1 inch larger than your baking dish.

Pour the apple mixture into the prepared dish and dot with the pieces of butter. Place the dough over the top of the apple filling and seal the edges. Cut vents in the top of the crust to allow steam to escape while baking.

Bake for 10 minutes. Reduce the oven temperature to 375 degrees F and bake for another 30 to 40 minutes, or until the crust is lightly browned on the top and the apples are tender.

Tart cherry cobbler

Serves 10 to 12

Batter

8 tablespoons (1 stick) butter,
  melted
1 cup all-purpose flour
1 cup sugar
1/2 teaspoon cinnamon
1 teaspoon baking powder
1 cup milk

Filling

3 cups tart cherries, pitted
1 cup light brown sugar
1 tablespoon all-purpose flour

Preheat the oven to 350 degrees F.

Pour the melted butter into an 8 x 10-inch baking dish. In a separate bowl, stir together the flour, sugar, cinnamon, and baking powder. Add the milk and stir until well blended. Pour the batter into the pan over the melted butter. Do not stir.

In a mixing bowl, toss the cherries with the brown sugar and flour. Distribute the cherry mixture evenly over the batter. Do not stir.

Bake for 50 minutes to 1 hour, or until golden brown. A toothpick inserted in the middle should come out clean.

Old-fashioned blackberry cobbler

Serves 12 to 15

Pastry Dough

2 1/2 cups all-purpose flour

3 tablespoons sugar

1 teaspoon salt

1/2 cup shortening

8 tablespoons (1 stick) unsalted butter

1/2 cup cold water

Filling

2 tablespoons (1/4 stick) butter, for the baking dish

1 cup granulated sugar

2 tablespoons flour

1 tablespoon lemon zest

2 teaspoons fresh ground nutmeg

4 pounds fresh blackberries

Preheat the oven to 425 degrees F. Butter a 2-quart baking dish.

In a medium bowl, sift together the flour, 3 tablespoons sugar, and salt. Using a pastry blender or fork, cut in the shortening and butter until the mixture resembles coarse crumbs. Sprinkle cold water over the flour mixture and work the dough with your hands until it forms a ball. Refrigerate the dough for at least 30 minutes to chill it. Once the dough is chilled, roll the dough out onto a lightly floured surface to a 1/8-inch thickness.

In a large mixing bowl, combine the sugar, flour, lemon zest, and nutmeg. Add the fresh blackberries to the mixture and gently toss to coat the berries. Spoon the berry mixture into the baking dish and top with the pastry dough. Cut vents in the dough to allow the steam to escape during baking.

Bake for 25 to 30 minutes, or until the topping is golden brown and the fruit is bubbly. Remove from the oven and cool for 10 minutes. Serve warm.

Layered sweet potato cobbler

Serves 12 to 15

1 pie shell (see recipe, p. 36)

Filling
4 large sweet potatoes, peeled and
    sliced 1/2-inch thick (about 8 cups)
Lightly salted water, enough to
    cover potatoes
2 cups granulated sugar
4 tablespoons all-purpose flour

1 teaspoon fresh ground nutmeg
Juice of 1 orange
Zest of 1 orange
8 tablespoons (1 stick) butter

Topping
2 tablespoons milk
1 tablespoon granulated sugar

Place the sweet potato slices in a large saucepan and cover with the salted water. Bring the water to a boil, then reduce the heat to medium and simmer for 10 minutes, or until the potatoes are just tender but still firm. Drain all but 2 cups of the cooking liquid from the pan. Add the sugar, flour, nutmeg, orange juice, and zest to the cooking liquid and stir to combine. Add the butter and return the saucepan to the heat. Stir just until the sugar dissolves.

Preheat the oven to 400 degrees F. Layer the potato slices in the bottom of a 9 x 13-inch glass baking dish. Pour the syrup made from the cooking liquid over the sweet potato slices.

On a lightly-floured surface, roll the pie dough out to a 1/8-inch thickness. Cut the dough with a 3-inch biscuit cutter and lay the dough rounds on top of the sweet potato slices. Brush the top of the pastry with the milk and sprinkle with the granulated sugar. Bake for 30 to 35 minutes, or until the pastry turns light brown and the juices bubble up.

Serve warm with your favorite ice cream, or with Whiskey Butter Sauce (see recipe, p.191)

Cheesecakes
&
Layer Cakes

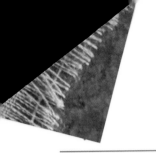

Sweet potato cheesecake

Serves 8 to 10

I wanted to create a fancy Southern version of a cheesecake, so I used two Southern staples—sweet potatoes and poundcake. The poundcake crust pairs nicely with the creaminess of the sweet potato filling. President Clinton tasted this on a visit to my store at the Auburn Avenue Curb Market, and loved it.

Poundcake Crust
6 to 7 (1/4-inch) slices Cream Cheese
    Poundcake (see recipe, p.57)

Cheesecake
2 cups (about 1 pound) sweet
    potatoes, mashed
3 (8-ounce) packages cream cheese

1 1/2 cups sugar
3 large eggs
1 cup half and half
1 teaspoon vanilla extract
1 teaspoon fresh ground nutmeg

Garnish
Fresh berries

Boil the sweet potatoes for 40 to 50 minutes, or until tender. Drain the potatoes, and run them under cold water to remove the skin. Mash the sweet potatoes in a bowl, set aside and allow them to cool completely.

Preheat the oven to 350 degrees F. Line the bottom of a 9-inch round cake pan with parchment and spray the sides with nonstick spray. Place the 1/4-inch slices of the Cream Cheese Poundcake in the bottom of the pan.

Beat the cream cheese until fluffy, gradually adding the sugar until it is well blended. Add the eggs one at a time, beating well after each addition. Stir in the mashed sweet potatoes. Add the half and half, vanilla and nutmeg and mix well.

Pour the mixture into the prepared pan and bake for 1 hour or until the center is almost set. Remove from the oven and allow the cheesecake to cool. When the cake is cool, run a knife along the edges and remove it from the pan by inverting it onto a plate. Then transfer the cheesecake to a serving platter, crust-side down, and refrigerate until ready to serve.

Garnish with fresh berries.

♡ Mississippi mud cheesecake

Serves 8 to 10

Crust
1 1/2 cups chocolate chip crumbs
4 tablespoons (1/2 stick) butter, melted

Filling
1 cup semi-sweet chocolate morsels
4 (8-ounce) packages cream cheese
1 1/2 cups sugar

4 eggs
2 teaspoons vanilla extract
1/2 teaspoon orange extract
1 cup half and half

Garnish
1/2 cup white chocolate, melted
1/2 cup milk chocolate, melted

Preheat the oven to 350 degrees F.

Combine the crumbs and butter in a bowl and press the crust evenly into the bottom of a lined 9-inch cake pan. Bake for 5 minutes, then remove from the oven and set aside.

To make the filling, melt the chocolate morsels in a double boiler. In a mixing bowl beat the cream cheese, adding the sugar gradually until it is well blended. Add the eggs one at a time, beating well after each addition. Stir in the melted chocolate, then add the vanilla, orange extract, and half and half and mix well.

Pour the filling into the prepared pan and bake for 50 minutes to 1 hour. Remove from the oven and allow the cheesecake to cool before transferring to a serving dish. Drizzle the top of the cake with the melted white and milk chocolate before serving.

Buttermilk vanilla cheesecake

Crust
6 to 7 (1/4-inch) slices Old-Fashioned
   Buttermilk Poundcake (see
   recipe, p. 54)

Filling
3 (8-ounce) packages cream cheese
1 1/3 cups, plus 2 tablespoons
   sugar, divided

3 eggs
1 1/3 cups buttermilk, divided
2 teaspoons pure vanilla extract

Preheat the oven to 350 degrees F. Line a 9-inch round cake pan with parchment paper and spray the sides with nonstick spray. Then line the pan with the 1/4-inch slices of the Old-Fashioned Buttermilk Poundcake.

Cream together the cream cheese and 1 1/3 cups sugar until smooth. Add the eggs one at a time, blending after each addition. Gradually stir in 1 cup buttermilk, then add the vanilla.

Pour the batter into the prepared pan and place the pan into a medium-size roasting pan. To create a water bath, pour enough water into the roasting pan to fill halfway up the sides of the cake pan. Bake the cheesecake for 50 minutes.

While the cheesecake is baking, cook the remaining buttermilk and 2 tablespoons sugar in a saucepan over medium heat, stirring occasionally, until the sugar dissolves completely.

Remove the cheesecake from the oven and pour the buttermilk mixture over the cake. Return the cake to the oven and continue to bake another 10 minutes. Allow the cake to cool before running a knife around the edges and transferring it from the pan to a serving dish.

Southern red velvet cake

Serves 12 to 16

Cake

2 1/2 cups all-purpose flour

1 1/2 cups sugar

1 teaspoon baking soda

1 teaspoon salt

2 tablespoons cocoa powder

1 1/2 cups vegetable oil

1 cup buttermilk, room temperature

2 large eggs, room temperature

6 tablespoons red food coloring

1 teaspoon white distilled vinegar

1 teaspoon vanilla extract

Cream Cheese Frosting

1 (8-ounce) package cream cheese, softened

4 cups powdered sugar, sifted

8 tablespoons (1 stick) unsalted butter, softened

1 teaspoon vanilla extract

Garnish

Crushed pecans, optiona[l]   *for Xmas*

Preheat the oven to 350 degrees F. Lightly oil and flour 3 (9 x [ ] cake pans.

In a large bowl sift together the flour, sugar, baking soda, salt, and cocoa powder. In a separate bowl whisk together the oil, buttermilk, eggs, food coloring, vinegar, and vanilla. In a standing mixer, mix the dry ingredients into the wet ingredients until the batter is smooth.

Divide the cake batter evenly among the prepared pans. Place the pans in the oven, evenly spaced apart. Bake for 30 minutes, rotating the pans after 15 minutes. Cakes should pull away from the sides of the pans and a toothpick inserted in the center should come out clean. Remove the cakes from the oven and run a knife around the edges to loosen them from the pans. Transfer the cakes to a wire rack, round side up, and allow them to cool completely.

To make the cream cheese frosting, use a mixer on low speed to cream the cheese, sugar and butter together until incorporated. Increase the speed to high and mix until fluffy, about 5 minutes, occasionally scraping down the sides of the bowl. Add the vanilla and mix again briefly until fluffy. Refrigerate the frosting until it stiffens somewhat before using.

To frost the cake, place a layer, rounded-side down, on a cake stand. Spread a 1/4- to 1/2-inch layer of cream cheese frosting over the top of the cake. Repeat with the other 2 layers, covering the sides of the cake after frosting the top layer. Garnish with the pecans and serve.

Lemon cheese layer cake

I used to bake this for one of my neighbors who was a very dear friend of the family. People are always confused about the lemon cheese—they ask me, "Where's the cheese?" The cheese refers to the texture of the lemon filling.

Cake
1 cup (2 sticks) unsalted butter, softened
2 cups sugar
4 eggs
3 cups unbleached all-purpose flour
2 1/2 teaspoons baking powder
1/2 teaspoon salt
1 cup half and half
2 tablespoons fresh squeezed lemon juice

Lemon Cheese
1 cup sugar
1 cup water
3 tablespoons all-purpose flour

5 egg yolks
1/2 cup fresh squeezed lemon juice
4 tablespoons (1/2 stick) butter
2 tablespoons lemon zest

Seven-Minute Frosting
1 1/2 cups sugar
5 tablespoons water
2 egg whites
1 tablespoon corn syrup
Pinch salt
1 teaspoon vanilla extract

Candied Lemon Zest
3 tablespoons lemon zest
1/2 cup sugar

Preheat the oven to 350 degrees F. Grease and flour 3 (9-inch) round cake pans.

Using a mixer, beat the butter at medium speed until creamy. Gradually add the sugar, beating until light and fluffy. Add the eggs one at a time, mixing well after each addition.

In another bowl, combine the flour, baking powder, and salt. Alternately add the flour mixture and the half and half to the creamed mixture, beginning and ending with the flour mixture. Mix well, then stir in the lemon juice and divide the batter evenly among the 3 pans.

Bake for 20 to 25 minutes, or until a toothpick inserted in the center comes out clean. Allow the layers to cool in the pans for 10 minutes, then transfer the cakes to a wire rack and let them cool completely.

While the cakes are baking and cooling, make the lemon cheese, seven-minute frosting, and the candied lemon zest.

To make the lemon cheese, combine the sugar, water, flour, egg yolks, and lemon juice in a saucepan and cook over medium heat, stirring constantly for 7 to 8 minutes, or until the mixture is thick enough to coat the back of a wooden spoon. Add the butter and stir until blended. Add the lemon zest. Allow the mixture to cool to room temperature before using, then refrigerate in a covered container.

To make the seven-minute frosting, combine the sugar, water, egg whites, corn syrup, and salt in the top of a double boiler. Beat with an electric mixer at medium speed until well blended. Place the pot over the double boiler, making sure that the top of the double boiler doesn't touch the simmering water. Beat constantly at high speed for 7 minutes, or until stiff peaks form and the mixture is glossy. Remove from the heat and stir in the vanilla.

To make the candied lemon zest, combine the sugar and zest in a bowl and toss gently to coat. Set aside for garnish.

To assemble the cake, spread the lemon cheese between the layers and on the top and sides of the cake. Fill a pastry bag fitted with a star tip with the frosting and pipe the frosting around the top and bottom of the cake to garnish, or as desired. Sprinkle the candied zest around the bottom of the cake, or as desired, and serve.

Italian cream cake

Serves 12 to 16

Cake
8 tablespoons (1 stick) butter
1/2 cup vegetable oil
2 cups sugar
5 egg yolks
2 cups flour
1 teaspoon baking soda
1 cup buttermilk
2 teaspoons vanilla extract
1 small can flaked coconut

1 cup chopped nuts of your choice
5 egg whites, stiffly beaten

Frosting
1 (8-ounce) package cream cheese
8 tablespoons (1 stick) butter,
   room temperature
1 box powdered sugar
1 teaspoon vanilla extract
1 cup nuts of your choice (optional)

Preheat the oven to 350 degrees F. Grease and flour 3 (9-inch) round cake pans.

Cream the butter and oil together. Add the sugar and egg yolks and beat well.

In a separate bowl, sift together the flour and baking soda, then alternately add the flour mixture and the buttermilk to the egg mixture. Stir in the vanilla, coconut, and nuts. Fold in the stiffly beaten egg whites. Divide the batter evenly among the 3 cake pans.

Bake for 25 minutes, or until a toothpick inserted in the middle comes out clean.

To make the frosting, mix the cream cheese, butter, powdered sugar, vanilla, and nuts together until well blended.

To frost the cake, place 1 layer, rounded-side down, on a cake stand. Spread a layer of cream cheese frosting over the top of the cake. Repeat with the other 2 layers, frosting the top layer before frosting the sides of the cake.

Caramel cake

Serves 12 to 16

Vanilla Cream Cake
1 cup (2 sticks) butter
2 cups sugar
4 eggs
3 cups cake flour
2 1/2 teaspoons baking powder
1/2 teaspoon salt
1 cup heavy cream
1 tablespoon pure vanilla extract

Caramel Icing
3 cups sugar, divided
3/4 cup half and half
1 egg
Pinch salt
8 tablespoons (1 stick) butter

Preheat the oven to 350 degrees F. Grease and flour 3 (9-inch) round cake pans.

Using a mixer at medium speed, cream the butter, gradually adding the sugar until the mixture is light and fluffy. Add the eggs one at a time, beating well after each addition.

In a separate bowl combine the cake flour, baking powder, and salt. Mixing at low speed, alternately add the flour mixture and the heavy cream to the batter, ending with the flour mixture. Stir in the vanilla.

Divide the batter among the 3 pans and bake for 35 minutes, or until a toothpick inserted in the center comes out clean. Allow the cakes to cool in the pans for 15 minutes, then transfer them to wire racks to cool completely.

To make the icing, cook 1 1/2 cups sugar in a heavy saucepan over medium heat, stirring constantly with a wooden spoon, until the sugar melts and becomes a golden-brown syrup.

In a separate bowl, combine the remaining 1 1/2 cups sugar, half and half, egg, salt, and butter and stir well. Add the half and half mixture to the saucepan and continue to stir. The mixture will be lumpy, so continue stirring until the mixture becomes smooth. Continue to cook over medium heat until the temperature reaches 230 degrees F on a candy thermometer, about 30 minutes. Remove from the heat and allow the caramel to cool for 10 minutes, stirring frequently, until it is smooth and creamy.

To assemble the cake, place 1 layer, rounded-side down, on a cake stand. Spread a layer of caramel icing over the top of the cake. Repeat with the other 2 layers, then ice the top layer and the sides of the cake.

Carrot cake

Cake
1 1/4 cups vegetable oil
2 cups granulated sugar
4 eggs
2 cups all-purpose flour
2 teaspoons baking soda
1 teaspoon baking powder
1/2 teaspoon salt
1 teaspoon cinnamon

3 cups (about 4 whole) carrots,
   peeled and grated
1 (8-ounce) can crushed pineapple
1 teaspoon vanilla extract

Frosting
1 (8-ounce) package cream cheese
1 pound powdered sugar
1 teaspoon vanilla extract
1/2 teaspoon lemon extract

Preheat the oven to 350 degrees F. Grease and flour 3 (9-inch) round cake pans.

Beat together the vegetable oil, sugar, and eggs until well combined. In a separate bowl sift together the flour, baking soda, baking powder, salt, and cinnamon. Add the flour mixture to the egg mixture and mix well. Drain the pineapple. Add the carrots and drained pineapple to the batter and mix until well blended.

Pour the batter evenly into the prepared cake pans. Bake for 30 minutes, or until a toothpick inserted in the center comes out clean. Turn the cakes out onto a wire rack and cool completely before frosting.

To make the frosting, mix the cream cheese, powdered sugar, vanilla and lemon extract until well combined. Spread the frosting over the top of each completely cooled layer as you stack them, reserving some frosting for the top and sides of the cake.

Hummingbird cake

Serves 12 to 16

Cake
3 cups all-purpose flour
2 cups granulated sugar
1/2 teaspoon salt
2 teaspoons baking soda
1 teaspoon ground cinnamon
3 eggs, beaten
1 1/4 cups vegetable oil
1 1/2 teaspoons vanilla extract
1 (8-ounce) can crushed pineapple,
  well drained
1 cup pecans, chopped

2 cups (3 to 4 whole) ripe bananas,
  sliced

Cream Cheese Frosting
1 (8-ounce) package cream cheese
8 tablespoons (1 stick) butter,
  room temperature
1 pound powdered sugar
2 teaspoons vanilla extract

Garnish
1/2 to 1 cup pecans, chopped

Preheat the oven to 350 degrees F. Grease and flour 3 (9-inch) round cake pans.

Sift together the flour, sugar, salt, baking soda, and cinnamon. Add the eggs and oil to the dry ingredients and stir with a wooden spoon until the dry ingredients are well moistened. Stir in the vanilla, pineapple, and pecans. Stir in the bananas just to combine.

Pour the batter evenly among the 3 pans and bake for 25 to 30 minutes, or until a toothpick inserted in the center comes out clean. Allow the cakes to cool in the pans for 10 minutes before turning out onto a wire rack to cool completely.

To make the cream cheese frosting, cream together the cream cheese and butter until smooth. Add the powdered sugar, beating with an electric mixer until light and fluffy. Stir in the vanilla.

To assemble the cake, place 1 layer, rounded-side down, on a cake stand. Spread a layer of the cream cheese frosting over the top of the cake. Repeat with the other 2 layers, frosting the sides of the cake after frosting the top layer. Sprinkle the top evenly with the chopped pecans and serve.

German chocolate cake

Serves 12 to 16

Cake
4 ounces Baker's German Sweet
  Chocolate
1/2 cup water
4 eggs, separated
2 cups flour
1 teaspoon baking soda
1/4 teaspoon salt
1 cup (2 sticks) butter, softened
2 cups sugar

1 teaspoon vanilla extract
1 cup buttermilk

Coconut-Pecan Frosting
4 egg yolks
1 (12-ounce) can evaporated milk
1 1/2 teaspoons vanilla extract
1 1/2 cups sugar
12 tablespoons (1 1/2 sticks) butter
2 2/3 cups flaked coconut
1 1/2 cups pecans, chopped

Preheat the oven to 350 degrees F. Cover the bottoms of 3 (9-inch) round cake pans with wax paper and spray the sides with cooking spray.

Combine the chocolate and water in a large microwavable bowl and heat on high in a microwave for 1 1/2 to 2 minutes, or until the chocolate is almost melted. Stir after 1 minute. Remove from the microwave and stir until the chocolate is completely melted. In a small bowl beat the egg whites on high speed until stiff peaks form. Set aside.

Mix the flour, baking soda, and salt together. In a separate bowl beat the butter and sugar until light and fluffy. Add the egg yolks one at a time, beating well after each addition. Blend in the melted chocolate and vanilla. Alternately add the flour mixture and the buttermilk to the chocolate mixture, blending after each addition. Add the egg whites and stir gently until well blended.

Pour the batter into the prepared pans and bake for 30 minutes, or until a toothpick inserted in the center comes out clean. Remove from the oven and allow the cakes to cool in the pans for 15 minutes, then transfer them to wire racks and remove the wax paper. Cool completely before frosting.

To make the frosting, whisk the egg yolks, milk, and vanilla in a large saucepan until blended. Add the sugar and butter and cook over medium heat for 12 minutes, stirring constantly, until the mixture is thick and golden brown. Remove form the heat and mix in the coconut and pecans. Allow the frosting to cool to room temperature.

To frost the cake, place 1 layer rounded-side down on a cake stand. Spread a layer of the coconut-pecan frosting over the top of the cake. Repeat with the other layers, frosting the sides of the cake after frosting the top layer.

Cooked chocolate layer cake

Serves 12 to 16

Cake
2 cups all-purpose flour
1 cup unsweetened cocoa powder
1 1/2 teaspoons baking soda
1/4 teaspoon salt
12 tablespoons (1 1/2 sticks) butter
1 cup brown sugar, packed
1 cup granulated sugar
3 large eggs

1 teaspoon vanilla extract
1 1/2 cups buttermilk

Cooked Chocolate Icing
5 cups sugar
1/3 cup cocoa powder
4 tablespoons (1/2 stick) butter
1 (15-ounce) can evaporated milk
1/2 cup whole milk
1 tablespoon vanilla extract

Preheat the oven to 350 degrees F. Grease 3 (8-inch) round cake pans and line the bottoms with wax paper. Grease the paper and dust the pans with flour.

Combine the flour, cocoa, baking soda, and salt and set aside.

In a large bowl beat the butter and sugars together until blended. With a mixer set on high, beat for 5 minutes, or until the mixture becomes pale and fluffy. Reduce the mixer speed to low and add the eggs one at a time, beating well after each addition. Add in the vanilla until just blended. Beat in the flour mixture alternately with the buttermilk, beginning and ending with the flour, until the batter is smooth.

Spoon the batter evenly among the pans. Space the pans evenly apart in the oven and bake for 22 to 25 minutes, or until a toothpick inserted in the center comes out clean. Allow the cakes to cool in the pans for 10 minutes, then run a knife around the edges to loosen the cakes, and invert them onto a wire rack. Remove the wax paper and allow the cakes to cool completely before icing.

To make the cooked chocolate icing, place the sugar and cocoa into a saucepan and mix well. Add the butter and milks and bring the mixture to a boil over medium-high heat. Boil for 4 minutes, stirring constantly, then lower the heat to a simmer and add the vanilla. Cook for another 7 to 10 minutes, stirring occasionally.

To assemble the cake, place 1 layer, rounded-side down, on a cake stand. Spread a layer of cooked chocolate icing over the top of the cake. The icing will be thin but will become firm as it cools. Repeat with the other 2 layers, covering the sides of the cake after icing the top layer. If the icing hardens while assembling the cake, set it over low heat and stir until it becomes loose enough to spread.

Lane cake

Serves 12 to 16

Cake

1 cup (2 sticks) butter, room
    temperature
2 cups sugar
3 1/2 cups all-purpose flour
3 1/2 teaspoons baking powder
1/2 teaspoon salt
1 cup milk
8 egg whites

Filling

8 egg yolks
1 cup sugar
1 cup (2 sticks) butter, room
    temperature
2 tablespoons brandy
2 tablespoons water
1/2 cup candied cherries, finely
    chopped
1 cup raisins, seeded and finely
    chopped
1 cup pecans, chopped

Preheat the oven to 350 degrees F. Grease and flour 4 (9-inch) round cake pans and line with greased wax paper.

Cream the butter and sugar together until it is light, fluffy, and smooth.

In a separate bowl, sift the flour with the baking powder and salt and add to the batter alternately with the milk, stirring until smooth. In a separate bowl beat the egg whites until stiff, then fold them into the cake batter.

Pour the batter into the prepared pans and bake for 20 minutes. Transfer the pans from the oven to a wire rack and let them stand 5 minutes before turning them out from the pans. Allow the cakes to cool completely before frosting with the filling.

To make the filling, place the egg yolks and sugar in a saucepan. Beat until well blended, then add the butter. While beating, cook over medium heat until the sugar dissolves and the mixture thickens. Remove from the heat and pour into a mixing bowl to cool slightly. Add the brandy and water, and stir in the fruits and pecans.

To frost the cake, place 1 layer, rounded-side down, on a cake stand. Spread a layer of the filling over the top of the cake. Repeat with the other 3 layers, fi-

Pineapple upside-down layer cake

Serves 12 to 16

People always seem to want more of a pineapple upside-down cake, so I decided to make it a layer cake. This is a great way to double up on an old-time favorite.

Topping

6 tablespoons (3/4 stick) butter, melted

1 1/2 cups brown sugar, firmly packed

12 slices fresh pineapple or 20 ounces crushed pineapple, drained

Maraschino cherries, as desired

Cake

1 cup (2 sticks) butter

1 cup sugar

2 eggs

3 cups all-purpose flour

3 teaspoons baking powder

1 teaspoon salt

1 cup milk

2 teaspoons vanilla extract

Garnish

1 cup pecans, chopped

Pour the melted butter evenly into 2 (9-inch) round cake pans, and sprinkle them with brown sugar. Arrange the pineapple and cherries decoratively over the sugar in both the pans.

Preheat the oven to 375 degrees F.

In a mixing bowl cream the butter, gradually adding the sugar and beating until light and fluffy. Add the eggs and beat well.

In a separate bowl, sift together the flour, baking powder, and salt and add to the creamed butter alternately with the milk, ending with the dry ingredients. Add the vanilla and beat until smooth.

Pour the batter evenly over the pineapple in the 2 prepared cake pans and bake for 35 minutes. Allow the cakes to cool for 5 minutes before turning out onto a serving plate. Stack the layers on top of one another and garnish with pecans, if desired. Serve with Homemade Whipped Cream (see recipe, p. 45).

Cookies, Muffins, & Quick Breads

Southern tea cakes

Yields 3 dozen

When I was growing up, our next door neighbor—a woman much older than my mother, as I remember— gave tea parties for me and my little sister, and she made these cookies for us. Use your own favorite cookie cutter.

1 cup sugar
1/4 cup buttermilk
1 egg
1/2 teaspoon baking soda
1/2 cup vegetable shortening

1/2 teaspoon salt
1/2 teaspoon vanilla extract
3 cups flour

Preheat the oven to 350 degrees F.

Mix together the sugar, buttermilk, egg, baking soda, shortening, salt, and vanilla. Add the flour, one cup at a time. Use enough flour to make the dough stiff, adding more flour if needed. Roll the dough out to approximately a 1/8-inch thickness and cut into desired cookie shapes. Bake for 15 to 20 minutes, or until cookies are brown around the edges.

Peanut butter cookies

Yields 2 dozen

8 tablespoons (1 stick) butter, room temperature
1/2 cup sugar, plus more for sprinkling
1/2 cup brown sugar, packed
1/2 cup peanut butter

1 egg
1 1/4 cups flour
3/4 teaspoon baking soda
1/2 teaspoon baking powder
Pinch salt

Preheat the oven to 375 degrees F.

Cream the butter, gradually adding the sugars. Mix in the peanut butter and the egg.

In a separate bowl, mix together the flour, baking soda, baking powder, and salt. Stir the dry ingredients into the butter mixture.

Drop tablespoon-sized cookies onto an ungreased cookie sheet about 3 inches apart. Sprinkle with sugar and use a fork to flatten the cookies in a crisscross pattern. Bake for 10 to 12 minutes, or until the cookies turn a light brown color. Cool on baking sheets, then transfer to a rack to cool completely.

Chocolate chip cookies

Yields 2 dozen

1 cup (2 sticks) butter, room temperature
3/4 cup granulated sugar
3/4 cup light brown sugar
1 egg
1/2 teaspoon salt
1 teaspoon baking soda

1/2 xcup unsweetened cocoa powder (optional)
2 1/2 cups flour
2 1/2 cups semisweet chocolate chips
1 cup walnuts (optional)
2 teaspoons pure vanilla extract

Preheat the oven to 375 degrees F.

Cream the butter and sugars together, then add the egg.

In a separate bowl, combine the salt, baking soda, cocoa, and flour and add this to the butter mixture. Fold the chocolate chips and walnuts into the dough and stir in the vanilla.

Bake for 12 minutes, or until the cookies turn golden brown.

Chocolate bourbon pecan bars

Yields 2 1/2 dozen

Bottom Crust
2 cups flour
1/2 cup sugar
1 cup (2 sticks) butter

Top Layer
1 cup corn syrup
4 tablespoons (1/2 stick) butter, melted

1 cup sugar
Pinch salt
1/4 cup cocoa powder
3 eggs, beaten
2 ounces bourbon
1 1/2 cups pecan pieces

Preheat the oven to 370 degrees F.

In a mixing bowl combine the flour and 1/2 cup sugar. Cut the butter into the flour mixture until it resembles coarse meal. Press the mixture into a pan and bake for 10 to 15 minutes. Remove the pan from the oven and reduce the heat to 350 degrees F.

In a separate mixing bowl, combine the corn syrup, butter, sugar, salt, and cocoa. Add the eggs, one at a time, and stir in the bourbon. Stir in the pecans.

Pour the mixture into the prepared pan. Bake at 350 degrees F for 30 to 40 minutes or until set. Remove from the oven, allow the bars to cool, and cut into squares to serve.

Chocolate fudge brownies with walnuts

Yields 1 dozen

1 cup (2 sticks) butter, melted
4 ounces unsweetened chocolate
   squares
2 cups sugar
4 eggs, beaten
1 teaspoon vanilla extract

1 1/2 cups flour
1/2 teaspoon salt
2 cups walnut pieces

Preheat the oven to 375 degrees F. Line a 9 x 13 x 2-inch pan with parchment.

Melt the butter and chocolate in a large bowl over a double boiler. Remove from the heat and stir in the sugar. Add the eggs and vanilla.

In a separate bowl, mix the flour and salt, then add it to the chocolate mixture. Stir in 1 cup walnuts. Pour the brownie mix into the prepared pan and sprinkle with the remaining walnuts.

Bake for 35 minutes and allow the brownies to cool before slicing.

Oatmeal raisin cookies

Yields 2 1/2 dozen

1 cup (2 sticks) butter, softened
3/4 cup white sugar
3/4 cup light brown sugar
2 eggs
1 teaspoon vanilla extract
2 cups all-purpose flour
2 1/2 cups rolled oats
1 teaspoon baking soda

1 teaspoon baking powder
1 teaspoon ground cinnamon
1/2 teaspoon salt
2 cups raisins

Preheat the oven to 375 degrees F.

In a large bowl, cream together the butter and both sugars until smooth. Beat in the eggs and vanilla until the batter is fluffy.

In a separate bowl, mix together the flour, oats, baking soda, baking powder, cinnamon, and salt and add this to the butter mixture. Stir in the raisins.

Drop tablespoon-sized balls of dough onto ungreased cookie sheets. Bake for 10 to 12 minutes, or until golden brown. Allow the cookies to cool on the baking sheets, then transfer them to a wire rack to cool completely.

Molasses sugar cookies

The molasses makes this a soft, chewy cookie. You use less sugar in this recipe, because the molasses adds sweetness.

3/4 cup shortening
1 cup white sugar, plus more for
   sprinkling
1 egg
1/2 cup molasses
2 cups all-purpose flour
2 teaspoons baking soda

1 teaspoon ground cinnamon
1/2 teaspoon salt

Cream together the shortening and sugar and beat until light and fluffy. Stir in the egg and molasses and beat well.

Sift together the flour, baking soda, cinnamon, and salt in a separate bowl and add to the wet ingredient mixture. Mix well.

Preheat the oven to 375 degrees F. Drop tablespoon-sized cookies onto a greased cookie sheet about 2 inches apart. Sprinkle the cookies lightly with sugar and bake for 8 to 10 minutes.

Buttery shortbread

Yields 6 dozen

1 cup (2 sticks) butter
2 cups flour
3/4 cup powdered sugar

Using an electric mixer, cream the butter until it is light and fluffy. With the mixer on low speed, gradually add the flour and powdered sugar. Allow the dough to chill for at least 30 minutes in the refrigerator.

Preheat the oven to 350 degrees F.

Once the dough is chilled, drop tablespoonfuls onto parchment-lined baking sheets.

Bake for 25 minutes or until the shortbread is nicely browned.

Sazerac tassies

The Sazerac is a traditional New Orleans cocktail made with anise liqueur. I based this dessert on the sazerac drink and made them small, bite-sized tassies (little tarts) because tassies pack a lot of flavor.

Filling

1 cup sugar

2 teaspoons flour

1/4 teaspoon baking powder

2 eggs, lightly beaten

4 tablespoons anise liqueur

2 teaspoons honey

Tart Shells

1 cup flour

2 ounces powdered sugar, plus
  more for dusting

1 teaspoon baking powder

12 tablespoons (1 1/2 sticks) butter

2 tablespoons anise seeds

To make the filling, combine the sugar, flour, and baking powder in a bowl. Add the beaten eggs, anise liqueur, and honey, and mix well.

To make the tart shells, combine the flour, powdered sugar, and baking powder in a mixing bowl. Cut the butter into the flour mixture with a pastry blender until the mixture resembles coarse meal. Use your hands to form a ball. Press the dough flat (but do not roll out) and cover with plastic wrap. Refrigerate the dough for at least 1 hour.

Preheat the oven to 375 degrees F. Once the dough has chilled, divide the dough into 24 balls and press each dough ball into a tart shell, or into the cups of mini muffin pans. Divide the anise seeds among the tart shells and spoon about 1 tablespoon of filling into each shell.

Bake the tassies for 15 minutes, or until lightly browned. Cool before you unmold the tassies from the tart pan.

Dust lightly with powdered sugar before serving.

Bourbon balls

1 (12-ounce) package fine vanilla
   wafer cookies, crushed
1 cup walnuts or pecans, chopped
1 cup powdered sugar, plus more
   to coat
2 tablespoons unsweetened cocoa
   powder, plus more to coat
1/4 cup bourbon

3 tablespoons light corn syrup
Coconut flakes, to coat

Combine the crushed vanilla wafers, chopped nuts, powdered sugar, and the cocoa powder in a mixing bowl.

In a separate bowl, combine the bourbon and light corn syrup. Add the bourbon mixture to the dry ingredients and mix well. Cover the mixture and refrigerate for at least 3 hours, or overnight.

Once chilled, form the dough into 1-inch balls. To coat, sift about 1 cup of powdered sugar onto a cookie sheet and roll the balls in the sugar until coated overall. Follow the same procedure to coat with cocoa powder, or the coconut flakes. Store in a sealed container until ready to serve. Bourbon balls will keep, refrigerated, for two weeks.

Sweet potato 'n molasses muffins

Yields 1 dozen

2 medium-sized sweet potatoes,
   cooked and mashed
1/2 cup molasses
1/2 cup vegetable oil
2 eggs
1 cup sugar

2 cups flour
1 teaspoon baking soda
1/2 teaspoon salt
1 teaspoon fresh ground nutmeg

Bake the sweet potatoes at 375 degrees F for 1 hour, or until tender. Allow the potatoes to cool, then peel, mash, and set them aside in a bowl.

Preheat the oven to 350 degrees F. Grease the bottoms of 12 muffin cups, or line the pan with paper muffin liners.

Combine the molasses, oil, and eggs and mix well. Add the mashed sweet potatoes and stir until well combined.

Combine the sugar, flour, baking soda, salt, and nutmeg in a separate bowl and add this to the sweet potato mixture. Stir together until just combined (the dough may look under-mixed). Spoon the batter into muffin cups and bake for 25 minutes, or until the muffins are firm to the touch.

♡ Naked hummingbird muffins

Yields 1 dozen

These muffins are based on my Hummingbird Cake recipe. They are "naked" be-cause they don't have the cream cheese icing—which makes them a great break-fast treat.

1 1/2 cups flour
3/4 cup sugar
1/4 teaspoon salt
1/2 teaspoon baking soda
1/2 teaspoon cinnamon
3/4 cup vegetable oil
1 large egg

1 cup (approximately 3) bananas, mashed
1/2 cup crushed pineapples, with liquid

Preheat the oven to 350 degrees F. Grease the bottoms of 12 muffin cups or line the pan with paper muffin liners.

In a mixing bowl, combine the flour, sugar, salt, baking soda, and cinnamon and mix well. In a separate bowl, combine the oil, egg, mashed bananas and pineapple. Make a well in the center of the flour mixture, pour the wet ingre-dients into the well and stir until the flour is just moistened. Spoon the batter into the prepared muffin cups and bake for 25 minutes, or until the muffins are firm to the touch.

Ginger pear muffins

Yields 1 dozen

Batter
2 1/2 cups all-purpose flour
1 teaspoon baking soda
1 teaspoon ground ginger
1/2 teaspoon salt
1/2 teaspoon cinnamon
1 3/4 cups brown sugar, packed
1/3 cup vegetable oil
2 eggs

1 cup buttermilk
2 cups (about 1 pound) pears,
 peeled and chopped

Topping
1/3 cup brown sugar, packed
2 teaspoons butter
1/4 teaspoon ground ginger

Preheat the oven to 375 degrees F. Grease 12 muffin cups or line a pan with paper muffin liners.

In a bowl, whisk together the flour, baking soda, ginger, salt, cinnamon, and sugar.

In a separate bowl, stir together the oil, eggs, and buttermilk. Fold the egg mixture into the dry ingredients, then add the pears and stir just until the dry ingredients are moistened. Spoon the batter into the prepared muffin cups.

To make the topping, combine the brown sugar, butter, and ginger in a bowl. Sprinkle the topping over the batter.

Bake until the muffin tops are firm to the touch, about 25 minutes.

♡ Spiced apricot jam muffins

Yields 1 dozen

2 1/2 cups all-purpose flour
1/2 cup granulated sugar
1 teaspoon baking powder
1/2 teaspoon salt
1/2 teaspoon baking soda
1/2 teaspoon ground ginger
1/2 teaspoon fresh ground nutmeg
2 eggs, lightly beaten

1 cup buttermilk
1/3 cup vegetable oil
12 tablespoons Apricot Jam (see recipe, p. 177)

Preheat the oven to 400 degrees F. Grease the bottoms of 12 muffin cups, or line a pan with paper muffin liners.

In a bowl, mix together the flour, sugar, baking powder, salt, baking soda, ginger, and nutmeg.

In a separate small bowl, mix the eggs, buttermilk, and oil. Using a spoon, make a well in the center of the flour mixture. Pour the egg mixture into the well and stir just until the flour mixture is moistened; the batter should still be a bit lumpy.

Gently spoon the batter into greased muffin cups, filling each 2/3 full. Spoon 1 tablespoon of the Apricot Jam into the center of each muffin.

Bake for 25 to 30 minutes or until the muffins are golden brown.

Blueberry muffins

Yields 1 dozen

2 eggs
1/2 cup vegetable oil
1 cup sugar
1 cup sour cream
2 1/2 cups flour, divided
1/2 teaspoon salt
1/2 teaspoon baking soda

1 teaspoon lemon zest
1 1/2 cups fresh blueberries

Preheat the oven to 400 degrees F. Grease 12 muffin cups, or line a pan with paper muffin liners.

In a large bowl, combine the eggs and oil and gradually beat in the sugar. Stir in the sour cream.

In a separate bowl, stir together 2 cups flour, the salt, baking soda, and lemon zest. Stir the dry ingredients into the sour cream mixture just until moistened. Toss the blueberries in the remaining flour and gently fold into the batter.

Spoon the batter into the prepared muffin cups and bake for 20 minutes, or until the muffins are firm to the touch.

Caramel banana nut muffins

Yields 1 dozen muffins, or 1 loaf

The combination of brown and white sugar adds extra flavor to this muffins.
The brown sugar caramel flavor goes great with bananas and allows you to
use less sugar in the recipe.

1/2 cup vegetable oil
1 cup light brown sugar, packed
2 eggs
1/4 teaspoon salt
1 teaspoon baking soda

2 cups flour
1 cup (approximately 3) bananas,
   mashed
1 cup walnuts, roughly chopped

Preheat the oven to 375 degrees F. Grease the bottoms of 12 muffin cups or a
loaf pan, or line a muffin pan with paper muffin liners.

In a large mixing bowl, stir together the oil and sugar. Add the eggs and beat
well.

In a separate bowl, sift the salt, baking soda, and flour together and add to
the egg mixture. Stir in the mashed bananas.

Pour the batter into a prepared muffin pan or a loaf pan, and sprinkle the
walnuts on top. Bake for 25 minutes, or until the muffins are firm to the touch.

♡ # Blackberry muffins

Yields 1 dozen

1 egg
1 cup buttermilk
1/2 cup vegetable oil
2 1/2 cups flour
3/4 cup sugar
1/4 teaspoon salt
2 teaspoons baking powder
1/2 teaspoon baking soda

1/4 teaspoon cinnamon
1 1/2 cups blackberries

Preheat the oven to 375 degrees F. Place the oven rack in the center position. Spray muffin cups with nonstick baking spray, or line with paper muffin cups and set aside.

In a bowl, mix together the egg, buttermilk, and oil.

In a separate bowl, combine the flour, sugar, salt, baking powder, baking soda, and cinnamon. Gently fold the blackberries into the dry mixture. With a rubber spatula, gently fold the wet mixture into the dry ingredients and stir just until combined.

Using two spoons or an ice cream scoop, fill each muffin cup almost full of batter. Bake for 25 minutes, or until the muffins are firm to the touch. Allow the muffins to cool before removing them from the pan.

Fig preserve snack cake

Yields 1 (9 x 13-inch) cake

1 1/2 cups sugar
2 cups all-purpose flour
1 teaspoon baking soda
1/2 teaspoon salt
1/2 teaspoon cloves
1 teaspoon fresh ground nutmeg
1 teaspoon cinnamon
3 eggs

1 cup vegetable oil
1 cup buttermilk
1 teaspoon vanilla extract
1 cup fresh Fig Preserves (see
   recipe, p. 174)

Preheat the oven to 350 degrees F. Grease and lightly flour a 9 x 13-inch baking pan.

In a mixing bowl, combine the sugar, flour, baking soda, salt, cloves, nutmeg, and cinnamon.

Combine the eggs and oil in a separate bowl and add them to the dry ingredients, stirring just until combined. Stir in the buttermilk and the vanilla, then add the preserves to the batter.

Pour the batter into the prepared pan and bake for 45 minutes, or until a toothpick inserted in the center comes out clean. Allow the cake to cool in the pan for 10 minutes, then remove it from the pan and let it cool completely before icing.

Spread the top and sides with Divine Caramel Sauce (see recipe, p.197) before serving.

Whole wheat apple muffins

Yields 1 dozen

1 cup whole wheat flour
1 cup all-purpose flour
1 teaspoon baking powder
1 teaspoon baking soda
1/4 teaspoon salt
2 teaspoon cinnamon
8 tablespoons (1 stick) unsalted
   butter, room temperature

3/4 cup light brown sugar
1 egg, lightly beaten
1 cup buttermilk
2 apples, peeled, cored, and chopped

Preheat the oven to 400 degrees F. Grease 12 muffin cups or line a pan with paper muffin liners.

Combine the flours, baking powder, baking soda, salt, and cinnamon in a mixing bowl.

In a separate bowl, cream the butter and add the sugar. Beat until light and fluffy. Add the egg and mix well. Stir in the buttermilk. Add the dry ingredients to the buttermilk mixture and fold in the chopped apples.

Spoon the batter into the prepared muffin pan and bake for 25 minutes, or until the muffins are firm to the touch. Allow the muffins to cool before serving.

Craisin bran muffins

Yields 1 dozen

3 tablespoons (3/8 stick) butter,
    room temperature
1/4 cup molasses
1 egg
1 cup bran cereal
1 cup buttermilk

1 cup all-purpose flour
1 teaspoon baking powder
1/2 teaspoon baking soda
1/4 teaspoon salt
3/4 cup craisins (sweetened, dried
    cranberries)

Preheat the oven to 375 degrees F. Grease 12 muffin cups or line a pan with paper muffin liners.

Beat together the butter and molasses. Add the egg and beat well. Stir in the bran cereal and buttermilk and let the batter stand for 5 minutes.

Sift together the flour, baking powder, baking soda, and salt in a mixing bowl. Add the wet mixture to the flour mixture and stir just until moistened. Stir in the craisins.

Fill the muffin cups about 2/3 full and bake for 25 minutes, or until the muffins are firm to the touch.

Strawberry-rhubarb muffins

Yields 1 dozen

1/3 cup vegetable oil
2 eggs
1/2 cup milk
2 cups flour, divided
1/2 cup sugar
2 1/2 teaspoons baking powder
1/2 teaspoon cinnamon

1 cup strawberries, sliced
1 cup (about 1/3 pound) rhubarb,
  diced

Preheat the oven to 375 degrees F. Grease 12 muffin cups, or line a pan with paper muffin liners.

In a large bowl, combine the oil, eggs, and milk.

In a separate bowl, stir together 1 1/2 cups flour, the sugar, baking powder, and cinnamon. Add the dry ingredients to the liquid mixture.

Toss the strawberries and rhubarb in the remaining 1/2 cup flour. Fold the fruit into the flour mixture. Fill the prepared tins with the batter and bake for 25 to 30 minutes, or until the muffins are firm to the touch.

♡ Buttermilk cornbread muffins

Yields 1 dozen

1 1/2 cups cornmeal
1/2 cup flour
2 tablespoons sugar
2 teaspoons baking powder
1 teaspoon baking soda
1/2 teaspoon salt
2 eggs

1 cup buttermilk
1/4 cup vegetable oil

Preheat the oven to 400 degrees F. Grease 12 muffin cups, or line a pan with paper muffin liners.

Combine the cornmeal, flour, sugar, baking powder, baking soda, and salt in a mixing bowl. Make a well in the center of the dry ingredients and add the eggs, buttermilk, and oil. Stir together just until combined. Pour the batter into the muffin cups.

Bake for 18 to 20 minutes, or until the muffins have risen and have begun to turn golden brown on the top.

Sweet potato angel biscuits

Yields 2 1/2 dozen

1 cup (2 medium-size) sweet
   potatoes, cooked and mashed
1 package dry yeast
1/4 cup warm water
2 1/2 cups flour
1 teaspoon baking powder
1 teaspoon salt
1/2 cup sugar

1/4 teaspoon cayenne pepper
1/2 teaspoon fresh ground nutmeg
1/2 cup shortening

Bake the sweet potatoes at 375 degrees F for 1 hour, or until tender. Allow the potatoes to cool, then peel and mash them. Set the potatoes aside in a bowl and keep them warm.

Combine the yeast and warm water in a small bowl and let stand for 5 minutes.

In a separate bowl, combine the flour, baking powder, salt, sugar, cayenne, and nutmeg. Cut in the shortening with a pastry mixer or fork until the dough is crumbly. Add the yeast mixture and sweet potatoes, stirring just until the dry ingredients are moistened.

Turn the dough out onto a lightly-floured surface and knead for 5 minutes. Place in a lightly greased bowl, turning the dough to grease it on all sides. Cover and refrigerate the dough for 1 hour, or overnight.

Once the dough is chilled, preheat the oven to 400 degrees F. Roll out the dough to a 1/2-inch thickness and cut with a 2-inch round biscuit cutter. Place the biscuits on ungreased baking sheets, cover, and let the dough rise in a warm place for 20 minutes, or until it has doubled in size.

Bake for 10 to 12 minutes or until the biscuits are lightly browned.

Grandma Ella's pure cane syrup sweet bread

Serves 10 to 12

My mother's mother used to make this recipe for my mom when she was growing up on their farm in the Florida panhandle. They used eggs from the hen house, and locally made cane syrup. This simple bread is good for a quick snack or as dessert, as it was originially enjoyed by farmers.

1 cup (2 sticks) butter, room
   temperature
2 cups pure cane syrup
1 teaspoon vanilla extract
3 eggs
2 cups all-purpose flour
Pinch salt

1 teaspoon baking soda
1 cup buttermilk

Preheat the oven to 350 degrees F. Grease an 11-inch cast-iron skillet.

Cream the butter and gradually add the cane syrup and vanilla. Add the eggs one at a time, blending well after each addition.

In a separate bowl, combine the flour, salt, and baking soda. Add the flour mixture and the buttermilk alternately to the syrup mixture, starting and ending with the flour. Pour the batter into the prepared skillet and bake 35 to 45 minutes, or until a toothpick inserted in the center comes out clean. Serve warm.

Caramel cornbread

Serves 8 to 10

2 tablespoons vegetable oil
2 cups white cornmeal
2 cups white sugar
1/2 cup light brown sugar, firmly
 packed
2 teaspoons baking powder
1 teaspoon salt
2 eggs, lightly beaten

2 cups buttermilk
8 tablespoons (1 stick) butter,
 melted

Preheat the oven to 450 degrees F. Place the vegetable oil in a 10-inch cast-iron skillet and place the skillet in the oven for 7 to 10 minutes.

In a large mixing bowl, combine the cornmeal, both sugars, the baking powder, and salt. Set aside.

In a separate bowl, combine the eggs, buttermilk, and butter and stir well. Add the egg mixture to the flour mixture, stirring just until the dry ingredients are moistened. (The batter will look under-mixed.)

Remove the hot skillet from the oven. Spoon the batter quickly into the skillet—you should be able to hear the batter sizzle as it hits the skillet. Bake for 25 minutes, or until the cornbread is golden brown. Remove the skillet from the oven and allow the cornbread to cool slightly before serving.

Serve warm with Fig Butter (see recipe, p. 174)

Cast-iron skillet cornbread

3 tablespoons vegetable shortening,
  or bacon grease
2 cups cornmeal
2 teaspoons baking powder
2 tablespoons sugar
2 teaspoons salt
2 cups buttermilk

2 eggs, beaten
2 tablespoons (1/4 stick) butter,
  melted

Preheat the oven to 425 degrees F. Coat a 9-inch cast-iron skillet with shortening or bacon grease and place in the preheated oven.

In the meantime, combine the corn meal, baking powder, sugar, and salt in a mixing bowl. Make a well in the center of the dry ingredients and add the buttermilk, beaten egg, and melted butter. Stir just until combined.

Remove the skillet from the oven. Pour the cornmeal batter into the hot skillet and return it to the oven. Bake for 25 minutes or until a toothpick inserted in the center comes out clean.

Hot water gingerbread

Serves 6 to 8

1/2 cup shortening
2/3 cup boiling water
1 cup molasses
1 egg, beaten
2 3/4 cups flour
1 1/2 teaspoons baking soda
1/2 teaspoon salt
1 1/2 teaspoons ginger

1 teaspoon cinnamon
1/4 teaspoon cloves
4 tablespoons (1/2 stick) butter,
 melted

Preheat the oven to 350 degrees F.

In a mixing bowl, melt the shortening in the boiling water. Stir in the molasses and egg.

Combine the flour, baking soda, salt, ginger, cinnamon, cloves, and butter in a separate bowl, then add this to the molasses mixture.

Pour the batter into a greased, or lined, 9-inch pan. Bake for 30 to 35 minutes, or until a toothpick inserted in the center comes out clean. Allow the gingerbread to cool before inverting the baking pan onto a serving platter.

To serve, cut into 6 to 8 portions and top each with a dollop of Tart 'n Tangy Lemon Sauce (see recipe, p.194).

Sweet cream biscuits

Yields 1 dozen

2 cups unbleached all-purpose flour
1/2 teaspoon salt
1 tablespoon baking powder
4 tablespoons sugar, plus more for
　　sprinkling
8 tablespoons (1 stick) unsalted

butter, plus more
　for brushing top of biscuits
1 cup heavy cream

Preheat the oven to 450 degrees F.

Combine the flour, salt, baking powder, and sugar in a large bowl. Cut the butter into the flour mixture using a pastry mixer or your fingers until it resembles a coarse meal. Add the cream, stirring until the flour mixture is just moistened and holds together. Scrape the dough from the sides of the bowl and turn it out onto a lightly floured surface.

Knead the dough gently 8 to 10 times with your hands. Form the dough into a ball and roll it out to a 1/2-inch thickness. Cut 12 biscuits using a floured, 2-inch biscuit cutter. Place the biscuits onto a baking sheet so their sides touch one another. Sprinkle the tops of the biscuits with sugar and bake for 10 to 12 minutes, or until browned. Remove the biscuits from the oven and brush with melted butter.

Buttermilk cathead biscuits

These get their name because they are said to be as big as a cat's head—they bake up about 4 inches wide, a great size for making breakfast sandwiches. They also pair perfectly with smoked sausage or other breakfast meats.

2 1/2 cups all-purpose flour
1/2 teaspoon salt
1/4 teaspoon baking soda
1 tablespoon baking powder
1 to 1 1/2 cups buttermilk
6 tablespoons shortening
Butter, melted, for brushing over
   biscuits

Preheat the oven to 450 degrees F.

In a mixing bowl, combine the flour, salt, baking soda, and baking powder. Cut in the shortening, using your fingers or a pastry cutter, until the flour mixture has the consistency of course-ground cornmeal. Make a well in the center of the dry mixture and add the buttermilk. Stir the mixture until the buttermilk is fully incorporated. Turn the dough out onto a lightly floured surface and knead carefully a couple of times.

To make the cathead biscuits, pinch off a 3-inch ball of dough and mold a slightly rounded ball. Place the biscuits onto an ungreased baking pan. Bake for 15 to 18 minutes, or until the tops of the biscuits turn a light golden brown. Remove from the oven and brush with melted butter.

Jams, Jellies,
Butters,
& Sauces

Blackberry jam

Yields 6 cups

2 quarts fresh blackberries
1 cinnamon stick
6 cups sugar

Wash the berries and place them in a saucepot with the cinnamon stick. Cook in a large saucepan over moderate heat until the berries are soft and their juices begin to flow. Remove the cinnamon stick.

Run the mixture through a sieve or food mill to obtain the juice and pulp. Measure out 4 cups of the juice and pulp mixture and place in a large, heavy saucepot. Bring the mixture to a boil and add the sugar. Lower the heat to medium and continue to cook until a candy thermometer reads 220 degrees F, about 30 minutes. Pour the mixture into jars and seal. Store the jam in the refrigerator until ready to use. The jam will keep in the refrigerator for up to 3 weeks.

If you wish to store the jam for a longer period of time, place the jars in a water bath for 10 minutes, then transfer to the counter to cool before storing in a cool, dry, dark place.

Fig preserves

Yields 2 cups

2 cups fresh figs, finely chopped
1 1/2 cups sugar

Combine the figs and sugar in a bowl. Cover and refrigerate overnight. Cook the mixture over low heat for 25 to 30 minutes, or until soft and thick. Remove from the heat and allow the preserves cool to room temperature. Store the preserves in a covered container in the refrigerator until ready to use. The preserves will keep in the refrigerator for up to 3 weeks.

Fig butter

Yields 1 1/2 cups

1 cup (2 sticks) butter, softened
1/2 cup fresh Fig Preserves

In a mixing bowl, beat the butter at medium speed until creamy. Add the Fig Preserves, stirring gently to combine. Store the butter in a covered container in the refrigerator until ready to use. The butter will lkeep in the refrigerator for up to 3 weeks.

Damson plum preserves

3 pounds Damson plums
½ cup water
6 cups sugar

Wash the plums and place them in a saucepot. Add the water and bring to a boil over medium heat, stirring constantly. Cook the plums for 10 to 15 minutes, or until the skins come off easily and the pits are released. Remove the pot from the heat and allow the mixture to cool enough in the pot to remove only the pits with your fingers. Discard the pits.

Stir in the sugar and place the pot back on the heat. Cook for 20 to 30 minutes more, stirring constantly.

Remove the pot from the heat and allow it to cool. Test the preserves' doneness by placing a teaspoon of preserves onto a plate. Place the plate in the freezer for 3 to 4 minutes to cool, then run your finger through the center of the preserves. If the preserves run back together, they aren't done and should cook longer. If the preserves remain parted where you ran your finger through, then they are ready. Store the preserves in a covered container in the refrigerator until ready to use. The preserves will keep in the refrigerator for up to 3 weeks.

If you plan to store the preserves for a longer period of time, place the preserves into sterilized jars and seal tightly. Place the jars in a water bath for 10 minutes, then transfer the jars to the counter to cool before storing in a cool, dry, dark place.

Apricot jam

Yields 10 to 12 cups

2 quarts apricots, peeled and
  crushed
6 cups sugar
1/4 cup fresh squeezed lemon juice

Blanch the apricots to remove the skins by dipping the apricots in a pot of boiling water for 2 minutes. Immediately remove the apricots to a sink or large
bowl filled with ice water to stop the cooking. Slip the skins off before slicing the
apricots in half and removing the pits.

In a large pot, combine the apricots, sugar, and lemon juice. Stir until the
sugar dissolves. Over high heat, bring the mixture to a boil, stirring constantly.
Once the apricots are tender, mash them with a potato masher in the pot. Cook
the mixture rapidly until it reaches the gelling point, when a candy thermometer reads 220 degrees F.

Store in a covered container in the refrigerator until ready to use. The jam
will keep in the refrigerator for up to 3 weeks.

Peach butter

Yields 4 cups

10 large fresh peaches, washed,
   pitted and sliced
1 cup water
2 cups sugar

Combine the peaches and water in a saucepan and bring to a boil. Reduce the heat to a simmer and cook the peaches until they become soft, 15 to 20 minutes. Run the peaches through a sieve to remove the skin and create a smooth texture. Return the peaches to the saucepan, stir in the sugar and cook over medium-low heat, stirring frequently, for 1 to 2 hours or until thick and smooth.

Remove the mixture from the heat. Spoon the butter into a covered container and store in the refrigerator for up to 3 weeks.

If you wish to store the butter longer, spoon the mixture into hot, sterile jars, leaving 1/4 inch of headspace. Cover the jar with sterilized lids and rings. Place the jars in a water bath for 10 minutes, then transfer them to the counter to cool before storing them in a cool, dry, dark place.

Strawberry jam

2 pounds fresh strawberries
4 cups sugar
1/4 cup fresh squeezed lemon juice
1 cinnamon stick

Wash and hull the strawberries. In a saucepan, crush the strawberries and stir in the sugar and lemon juice. Add the cinnamon stick and stir over low heat until the sugar is dissolved.

Increase the heat to high and bring the mixture to a rolling boil. Using a large spoon, skim off any foam that forms on the surface. Continue to boil, stirring often, until the mixture is thickened and a candy thermometer reads 220 degrees F, about 30 to 40 minutes. Remove the cinnamon stick.

Transfer the jam to a covered container and refrigerate until ready to use. The jam will keep in the refrigerator for up to 3 weeks.

If you wish to store the jam for a longer period of time, spoon the jam into hot, sterile jars and seal. Place the jars in a water bath for 10 minutes and transfer them to the counter to cool before storing them in a cool, dry, dark place.

Orange marmalade

Yields 8 to 10 cups

6 large oranges
1 lemon
6 cups water
8 cups sugar

Peel the oranges and lemon, retaining the peels. Slice the peels very thinly. Cut up the orange and lemon pulps and remove any seeds. Combine the pulp and thinly sliced peels in a large pot and add the water. Bring the mixture to a boil, stirring frequently. Add the sugar and simmer about 10 minutes, or until the sugar dissolves. Remove from the heat and allow the mixture to stand overnight in a cool place.

The next day, bring the mixture to a boil again and simmer until the peel is tender. Skim off the scum that forms on top. Cook rapidly, stirring constantly, for 30 minutes or until a candy thermometer reads 220 degrees F. Pour the mixture into hot, sterilized jars and seal. Store the marmalade in the refrigerator until ready to use. The marmalade will keep in the refrigerator for up to 3 weeks.

If you wish to store the marmalade for a longer period of time, place the jars in a water bath for 10 minutes, then transfer to the counter to cool before storing in a cool, dry, dark place.

Apple jelly

This jelly is perfect paired with the Old-Fashioned Pork Cake. It adds just the right amount of sweetness to complement the cake.

8 pounds apples
10 cups water
3 to 4 cinnamon sticks
6 cups sugar

2 tablespoons fresh squeezed
lemon juice

Rinse the apples and cut them into coarse chunks. Place the apple chunks, along with the cores and seeds, into a very large stockpot. Add the water and cinnamon sticks, cover, and bring to a boil. Reduce the heat to a simmer and leave the lid askew to allow steam to escape from the pot. Cook for 15 to 20 minutes, or until the apples are tender.

Line a mesh colander with a piece of muslin cloth or a few folds of cheesecloth (or use a jelly bag and stand) and set the colander over a deep bowl. Ladle the apples and the liquid into the colander. Remove the cinnamon stick and let the apples stand overnight. Do not press down on the apples at any time to extract more juice, or the jelly will become cloudy.

The next day, pour the juice into a stockpot fitted with a candy thermometer. Stir in the sugar and lemon juice and bring the mixture to a boil. Remove any scum that forms on the surface. Cook until the mixture reaches 220 degrees F, then remove from the heat.

Test the jelly's doneness by placing a teaspoon of the jelly onto a plate. Place the plate in the freezer for 3 to 4 minutes to cool, then run your finger through the center of the jelly. If the jelly wrinkles and holds its shape, it's done. If not, continue cooking the jelly and re-test it periodically until it is done.

Remove the pot from the heat, ladle the jelly into sterilized jars and seal tightly. Store the jelly in the refrigerator until you are ready to use it. The jelly will keep in the refrigerator for up to 3 weeks.

If you wish to store the jelly for a longer period of time, place the jars in a water bath for 10 minutes, then transfer to the counter to cool before storing in a cool, dry, dark place.

Sweet potato butter

8 cups (about 4 pounds) sweet
   potatoes, diced and peeled
4 cups water
2/3 cup orange juice concentrate
1/2 cup dark brown sugar, packed
1 teaspoon fresh ground nutmeg

In a heavy saucepan, combine the sweet potatoes, water, orange juice concentrate, brown sugar, and nutmeg. Mix well and bring the mixture to a boil. Reduce the heat and simmer, stirring occasionally, for about 1 1/2 hours or until the mixture has thickened and only about 1 cup of liquid remains.

In a blender, process the mixture in batches until smooth. Transfer the butter to jars or covered containers. Chill the butter for at least 2 hours before serving.

The butter may be stored in the refrigerator in a covered container for up to three weeks.

Blueberry jam

Yields 5 cups

2 cups blueberries
4 cups sugar
1/4 cup fresh squeezed lemon juice

Cook the blueberries and sugar together in a large, heavy saucepan over medium heat for 25 to 30 minutes, or until a candy thermometer reads 220 degrees F and the jam slides off the side of a spoon in sheets.

Once the jam is 220 degrees F, add the lemon juice and cook a few minutes more, or until the jam re-thickens. Pour the jam into sterilized jars and seal.

Store the jam in the refrigerator until ready to use. The jam will keep in the refrigerator for up to 3 weeks.

If you wish to store the jam for a longer period of time, place the jars in a water bath for 10 minutes, then transfer to the counter to cool before storing in a cool, dry, dark place.

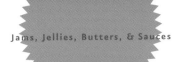

Brandied apricot glaze

Yields 1 1/2 cups

Making a glaze with spirits will make a big difference—it adds a little something special to your dessert.

10 ounces Apricot Jam (see recipe, p. 177)
1 teaspoon ginger, freshly grated
3 ounces brandy

Cook the Apricot Jam in a saucepan over medium heat until melted. Remove from the heat, add the ginger and allow the mixture to cool slightly. Add the brandy and cool the glaze to room temperature. Serve with Old-Fashioned Buttermilk Poundcake.

Molasses glaze

Yields 1/3 cup

1 cup powdered sugar, sifted
2 tablespoons molasses
1/4 teaspoon fresh ground nutmeg

Combine the powdered sugar, molasses, and nutmeg in a small bowl. Mix until the sugar is completely absorbed and the glaze is smooth. Serve with Sweet Potato Poundcake.

Lemon glaze

♡

Yields 1/3 cup

1 cup powdered sugar
2 tablespoons fresh squeezed
  lemon juice
1 teaspoon lemon zest

Combine the powdered sugar, lemon juice and zest in a bowl and mix until smooth. Serve with Sour Cream Poundcake.

Chocolate glaze

♡

Yields 1 cup

1/4 cup semisweet chocolate chips
3 tablespoons (3/8 stick) butter
1 tablespoon light corn syrup
1/2 teaspoon vanilla extract

In the top of a double boiler, combine the chocolate chips, butter, and corn syrup. Stir until the chips are melted and the mixture becomes smooth. Remove the double boiler from the heat and stir in the vanilla. Drizzle the warm glaze over the top of the Chocolate Buttermilk Poundcake and serve.

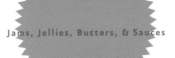

Whiskey butter sauce

This is a light butter that will melt into a sauce when served over warm desserts. Whiskey Butter Sauce is great with many desserts, including the Cinnamon Raisin Bread Pudding and the Fresh Peach Cobbler.

8 tablespoons (1 stick) butter,
  softened
2 cups powdered sugar
1 tablespoon hot water
2 tablespoons whiskey

Cream together the butter and sugar in a mixing bowl. Add the water and stir until combined. Stir in the whiskey. Spoon the sauce into a container and cover. Refrigerate until ready to serve.

Buttered rum sauce

Yields 1 2/3 cups

1 cup sugar
1/2 cup water
8 tablespoons (1 stick) butter
2 ounces dark rum

Bring the sugar and water to a rolling boil, stirring continuously. Remove from the heat. Whisk in the butter until silky, about 1 minute. Remove the mixture from the stovetop and stir in the rum. Continue to stir until cool enough to pour into a container. Serve warm over Cinnamon Raisin Bread Pudding or Rich's Rum Poundcake.

Tart 'n tangy lemon sauce

Yields 1 cup

1 cup sugar

1 egg, beaten

1 tablespoon lemon zest

4 tablespoons fresh squeezed
lemon juice

2 tablespoons (1/4 stick) butter,
softened

Combine the sugar, egg, lemon zest, and lemon juice in a double boiler. Bring the mixture to a boil, then reduce the heat to a simmer. Cook, stirring constantly for 8 to 10 minutes, or until the sauce thickens. Remove the double boiler from the heat and stir in the butter.

Serve with Hot Water Gingerbread.

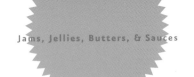

Divine caramel sauce

2 cups light brown sugar
1 (14-ounce) can sweetened
  condensed milk
8 tablespoons (1 stick) butter
1/2 cup milk
1 teaspoon vanilla extract

Combine the sugar and condensed milk in a medium saucepan and stir until well blended. Cook over medium heat, stirring constantly, until the sugar dissolves. Remove from the heat and add the butter, stirring well. Add the milk and vanilla, stirring to combine. Let the sauce cool to room temperature. Store the sauce in a covered container until ready to use. Serve with Fig Preserve Snack Cake, or your favorite vanilla ice cream.

Nutmeg sauce

Yields 1 cup

1 cup water
/2 cup sugar
1 tablespoon cornstarch
1 teaspoon fresh ground nutmeg
2 tablespoons (1/4 stick) butter

In a large saucepan bring the water to a boil.

In a mixing bowl, combine the sugar, cornstarch, and nutmeg. Mix well.

Gradually stir 1/2 cup boiling water into the sugar mixture. Add the sugar mixture to the remaining boiling water in the saucepan. Continue cooking for 5 to 8 minutes, or until the sauce thickens. Remove the saucepan from the heat and stir in the butter.

Store the sauce in a covered container until ready to use. Serve with Cinnamon Raisin Bread Pudding, Fresh Peach Cobbler, or poundcakes.

Index

Index

Acknowledgments

I am most grateful to my son, Robert (Bobby) W. Jones Jr., who unselfishly placed his music on semi-hiatus and stepped into the fulltime role of the day-to-day operations of running the bakery… while mommy wrote her first cookbook.

I appreciate the assistance given to me by Susan Williams, invaluable kitchen assistant and chief recipe tester. And many thanks to Annette Joseph for her beautiful food styling, and for the use of her home and kitchen to photograph this book.

Acknowledgments

I am indebted to Ms. Edna Lewis, mentor and friend, for the countless hours spent together teaching and discussing the art of Southern cooking; and for introducing me to the book *What Mrs. Fisher Knows About Old Southern Cooking.*

Special thanks to Janice Shay of Pinafore Press, first of all for her belief in the project, and for her guidance and support throughout the task of bringing my vision of Southern heritage recipes to print.